the
All-Sufficient
CHRIST :
studies in Colossians

by Theodore H. Epp

Director

Back to the Bible Broadcast

A
BACK TO THE BIBLE
PUBLICATION

Back to the Bible

Lincoln, Nebraska 68501

70,000 printed to date—1982
(5-0856—70M—82)
ISBN 0-8474-1190-7

Printed in the United States of America

Foreword

For several years Theodore H. Epp has wanted to bring a radio series on Colossians and have it published in book form. However, he never felt he quite had the grasp of the main theme of Colossians needed to produce such a series. The various commentaries he read seemed to stress that the main purpose of Colossians was to answer the false teachers in Colossae. Although Mr. Epp knew that a proper understanding of Colossians would give answers to false teaching, he was convinced that the book was somehow intended to meet the personal needs of individual believers.

Then, while reading in the *New International Version* for his own devotions, Mr. Epp gained new insights. He was more forcibly impressed than ever before that the purpose of Colossians was to show believers the all sufficiency of Christ, not just to answer false teaching. With this new impetus, Mr. Epp began seriously studying Colossians with a future series in mind. That study took him nearly one and a half years from beginning to end. He read Colossians 24 times in different translations and carefully studied what evangelical Bible scholars had written about the book.

Although 75 years of age with 50 years in the ministry, Mr. Epp did not take lightly the responsibility of presenting this series on Colossians to the public. In fact, he averaged over eight hours of work per message by the time he had prepared the messages, produced the radio programs and read the messages after they had been edited for this book.

This study is now placed in your hands. It emphasizes not only the doctrine of the Book of Colossians but also especially emphasizes the practice which is based on that doctrine. May this study give you a greater realization of what the Bible means when it says, "Christ in you, the hope of glory" (Col. 1:27).

—Harold J. Berry, Instructor
Grace College of the Bible
Omaha, Nebraska

Contents

Chapter 1

Colossians: A Panoramic View

Although the Book of Colossians is relatively short, it is
packed with significant spiritual truths. These truths primarily point to the all-sufficient Christ. A careful reading of
the Book of Colossians brings the supremacy of Christ into
clear view. This should cause the heart of each believer to
respond in worship as he realizes that Christ is all he needs.

The supremacy, or all-sufficiency, of Christ is seen throughout the Book of Colossians in such verses as 1:18,19: "And he
is the head of the body, the church: who is the beginning, the
firstborn from the dead; that in all things he might have the
preeminence. For it pleased the Father that in him should all
fulness dwell."

The supremacy of Christ is clearly seen in 2:3: "In whom
are hid all the treasures of wisdom and knowledge." From
this same chapter, notice especially verses 9 and 10: "For in
him dwelleth all the fulness of the Godhead bodily. And ye
are complete in him, which is the head of all principality and
power."

The all-sufficiency of Christ is also clearly evident from
3:11: "Where there is neither Greek nor Jew, circumcision
nor uncircumcision, Barbarian, Scythian, bond nor free: but
Christ is all, and in all."

From the preceding verses it is rather easy to conclude that
Colossians emphasizes that Christ is all we need. And
because of who He is, we are to give Him first place in all of
our consideration—He is to be preeminent in everything we
think and do.

This means that each of us who knows Jesus Christ as
Saviour should desire to know Him better so we might not
only recognize His all-sufficiency but might also honor and
please Him in all that we do. The Apostle Paul had the strong

7

desire to know Jesus Christ better. Paul expressed it in this manner: "That I may know him, and the power of his resurrection, and the fellowship of his sufferings, being made conformable unto his death" (Phil. 3:10).

From our own realm of acquaintances we realize that we know people on different levels, some to a greater depth than others. Recently, I was introduced to a person in a counseling situation. I had corresponded with the individual occasionally; so it was possible for me to say, "I know him." But I don't know that individual nearly as well as I know those I work with every day. Those of us who are married realize we become acquainted with the habits and characteristics of our spouses so well that we know them in a way we do not know others. I dated my wife for five years before we were married and knew her quite well during that time, but that was nothing in comparison to the way I know her now after having been married more than 50 years.

When we are with someone most of the time, we are able to tell changes in attitude from an inflection in the voice or some other characteristic. I am sure you have also found that those who are closely associated with you can tell when something is wrong, even though others might not detect it.

In the spiritual realm, we need to have a growing relationship with the Lord Jesus Christ. The more time we spend with Him in prayer and the reading of His Word, the more we will understand how He thinks. We need to get to know Him so well that we can think as He thinks and see as He sees and hear as He hears. Then He will be able to use us who are His children to do His will. But each of us needs to ask, "How well do I really know Him?"

The key to realizing the all-sufficiency, or supremacy, of Jesus Christ is to really learn to know Him—not only as Saviour but also as Lord. If you are interested in giving special attention to knowing Christ better, you will find the following passages very beneficial in this regard. Perhaps you could gradually work through them in your devotional times and then during the day think about the concepts in these passages. Some passages that would be possible for such a study are: Romans 11:33-36; II Corinthians 10:3-5; Ephesians 1:17-19; 4:11-15; Philippians 3:8; II Peter 1:2-8; 3:18 compared with II Timothy 1:12. A careful study of these passages will enable you to know Christ better because they emphasize all that He is to the believer.

Moses' Example

There are Old Testament examples of what it means to know God better. Moses was one who, in his early years, had a difficult time learning to know God. Exodus 1—5 reveals some of those difficult times.

However, there came a time in Moses' life when he understood God as he never had before, and from that time forward Moses was a different person. God made Himself known to Moses and to the Israelites at the time when Pharaoh was refusing to let them leave Egypt. God told Moses, "Wherefore say unto the children of Israel, I am the Lord, and I will bring you out from under the burdens of the Egyptians, and I will rid you out of their bondage, and I will redeem you with a stretched out arm, and with great judgments: and I will take you to me for a people, and I will be to you a God: and ye shall know that I am the Lord your God, which bringeth you out from under the burdens of the Egyptians. And I will bring you in unto the land, concerning the which I did swear to give it to Abraham, to Isaac, and to Jacob; and I will give it you for an heritage: I am the Lord" (Ex. 6:6-8).

Notice the expression "I am the Lord," which is mentioned three times in the above passage. This was God's way of emphasizing His all-sufficiency to Moses. In other words, God was saying, "I have the ability to do what I set out to do." Following that expression is a sevenfold statement of what the Lord would do, each statement beginning with the words "I will." God made it clear to Moses that He had the authority and the power to do whatever He chose to do.

After God had revealed Himself to Moses, "Moses spake so unto the children of Israel" (v. 9). Moses now seemed to understand that the deliverance of Israel from Egypt was really God's undertaking. God promised that He would work in such a way that it would be clear to the Egyptians that He was the Lord. God told Moses, "And the Egyptians shall know that I am the Lord, when I stretch forth mine hand upon Egypt, and bring out the children of Israel from among them" (7:5). Moses had to learn that God was sufficient for everything he needed, and this is the same lesson believers need to learn today.

Regrettably, many believers today seem to be seeking for something more than Jesus Christ. They feel they have to have some kind of exciting experience, some new doctrine, some new formula for success or some special sign. But Colossians 2:10 tells every believer, "Ye are complete in him, which is the head of all principality and power." One paraphrase of this verse reads: "Moreover, your own completeness is only realized in him, who is the authority over all authorities, and the supreme power over all powers" (Phillips).

The Book of Colossians tells us of the all-sufficiency of Christ and how to appropriate what we have in Him. It is not enough that Christ is all sufficient. If we are to personally benefit, we must take what we have in Him and apply it to our lives; that is, by faith appropriate Him in His sufficiency for all our insufficiencies. As we discover the fullness of Christ and apply these truths to our lives, we will no longer need special experiences or man-made regulations. These cannot take the place of, nor add to, the riches that the believer has in the Lord Jesus Christ.

A continuing burden of the Apostle Paul was that believers might realize the riches that are theirs in the Lord Jesus Christ. Thus, he prayed for the Ephesians—and all believers: "The eyes of your understanding being enlightened; that ye may know what is the hope of his calling, and what the riches of the glory of his inheritance in the saints, and what is the exceeding greatness of his power to us-ward who believe, according to the working of his mighty power" (Eph. 1:18,19). Just as the apostle himself wanted to know more about the Lord Jesus Christ (Phil. 3:10), so he prayed for others that they might know Christ better.

Colossians and Ephesians Compared

It is interesting to compare the Book of Colossians with the Book of Ephesians. These two books complement one another in many ways and are sometimes called "twin" letters, or epistles. Ephesians emphasizes the glory of the Church in its relationship to Christ. It emphasizes the Church as the Body of Christ. As such, Ephesians deals more with the life of the Body as the individual members derive their life from the Head (Christ). Such an emphasis enables the reader to see the Church in its eternal character and gives the believer an understanding of what his conduct ought to be as a member of the Body of Christ. The Church, as presented in Ephesians, is a heavenly people.

On the other hand, Colossians emphasizes the glory of Christ, who is the Head of the Body, the Church. Thus, Colossians emphasizes that the Church derives its life and power from Christ in order that He might live through its members and produce a conduct that is pleasing and honoring to God. In Colossians, the resources of the Church are revealed as being centered in Christ. This is especially stressed by Colossians 2:9,10: "For in him dwelleth all the fulness of the Godhead bodily. And ye are complete in him, which is the head of all principality and power."

So as we proceed through the Book of Colossians, we will expect to find an emphasis on the Person of Christ as the Head of the Church. May I encourage you to make it your prayer that you might see Christ as He really is and that you might be able to appropriate these great truths for your own life?

The Book of Colossians forms a part of the 66 books of the Bible, which are inspired by God. Therefore, what is said concerning inspired Scripture in II Timothy 3:16 applies to the Book of Colossians: "All scripture is given by inspiration of God, and is profitable for doctrine, for reproof, for correction, for instruction in righteousness." Notice four significant words in this verse—doctrine, reproof, correction, righteousness.

Doctrine and Practice

Doctrine, or teaching, is the standard of truth. Doctrine is not to be derived from tradition or from the institutional church but from the Scriptures. Doctrine derived from the Scriptures provides a basis for the Christian faith. Everything else must be examined to see how it compares with the truth presented in God's Word.

God did not intend, however, that the Bible be doctrine for doctrine's sake. There must also be reproof, correction and instruction in righteousness. When there are deviations from true doctrine, there must be reproof and correction. "Instruction in righteousness" actually refers to the training process as it relates to the doctrines of the Word of God.

Of the four chapters in the Book of Colossians, the first two relate primarily to doctrine. These chapters present the basic facts of Christ as the Head of the Church. Believers are seen as those who are a part of the Body of Christ, who have available to them all the fullness of Christ's life and power.

The last two chapters of the Book of Colossians relate primarily to practice. These chapters not only give reproof and correction but also instruction in proper Christian conduct.

This division of the Book of Colossians is seen from Paul's introductory remarks in chapter 1. Verse 9 relates to doctrine: "For this cause we also, since the day we heard it, do not cease to pray for you, and to desire that ye might be filled with the knowledge of his will in all wisdom and spiritual understanding."

Verses 10 and 11 relate to practice: "That ye might walk worthy of the Lord unto all pleasing, being fruitful in every good work, and increasing in the knowledge of God; strengthened with all might, according to his glorious power, unto all patience and longsuffering with joyfulness." This is basically the subject matter of chapters 3 and 4.

False Teachers

The church of Colossae was threatened by certain perils. False teachers had confused believers in that first-century church just as false teachers have confused believers today. Paul wrote this letter to the church of Colossae to instruct them in true doctrine so they might recognize the heresies of the false teachers. Paul did not minimize doctrine—he realized that the Colossians needed to know the truth concerning Jesus Christ. Even as indicated in II Timothy 3:16, Paul gave doctrine, but he also gave reproof, correction and instruction in righteousness.

In the church of Colossae, Christ was given a great and honorable place, but He was not given His rightful place. He was not given total supremacy in the daily lives of the believers. This same problem is also found in many believers today—we give Christ eminence, but we do not give Him preeminence. It is important that we recognize Him as the absolute, final authority and power in our lives.

Are you having a struggle placing Christ in first place in all of your thinking and activities? If so, I believe the message of the Book of Colossians will be very helpful to you even as it has been to me.

The intent of Paul's Colossian letter was to reveal Christ as the One who is absolutely supreme in everything, especially in our personal lives. This emphasis is especially seen in 1:18: "He is the head of the body, the church: who is the beginning, the firstborn from the dead; that in all things he might have the preeminence." Notice how other versions translate this verse: "He is also head of the body, the church; and He is the beginning, the first-born from the dead; so that He Himself might come to have first place in everything" (NASB). Another translation renders this verse: "And he is the head of the body, the church; he is the beginning and the firstborn from among the dead, so that in everything he might have the supremacy" (NIV).

As we will see in detail later, the teaching of Colossians may be summarized in the few words of 2:9,10: "For in him dwelleth all the fulness of the Godhead bodily. And ye are complete in him, which is the head of all principality and power." From 1:18 and 2:9,10, I am sure you can understand why I believe the theme of Colossians is "The All-Sufficient Christ." If we have the Lord Jesus Christ, what else do we need? We have what we need, not only for our salvation but also for our daily Christian walk. He has provided all things that are necessary for us, even as we are told in II Peter 1:3: "According as his divine power hath given unto us all things that pertain unto life and godliness, through the knowledge of him that hath called us to glory and virtue."

Notice that Paul's approach to solving the problem in Colossae was not by an outright attack on the false teachers. Instead, he attacked the false teaching. So often today I believe that well-meaning Christians take the wrong approach—they attack the teachers instead of the teaching.

Paul began by exalting Jesus Christ and showing His supremacy in all things. Then he had a basis by which he could show the false teaching to be incorrect. First he established truth; then he pointed out error. After refuting the heresies of the false teachers, Paul explained to believers that the greatest antidote to false teaching is a God-honoring life which is made possible through the all-sufficiency of the indwelling Christ.

You will notice as we progress through the Book of Colossians that Paul did not treat the subject of behavior until he treated the subject of correct doctrine. What we believe determines the way we behave; so it is of utmost importance to first establish what we believe.

For instance, if we properly believe that our bodies in themselves are not evil but are really temples, or dwelling places, of the Holy Spirit, we will behave accordingly. Although our bodies themselves are not evil, we all possess a sin nature which expresses itself by acts of sin—this is the evil that is to concern us.

Paul emphasized the proper perspective concerning the believer's body when he asked the Corinthians "What? know ye not that your body is the temple of the Holy Ghost which is in you, which ye have of God, and ye are not your own? For ye are bought with a price: therefore glorify God in your body, and in your spirit, which are God's" (I Cor. 6:19,20).

Wrong doctrine always leads to wrong living. However, right doctrine should lead to righteous living. It does not always do so, but it should. Some who believe properly refuse to apply what they believe, but the normal pattern is that right doctrine produces righteous living.

I believe this is why Paul emphasized correct doctrine in the first part of his letter to the Colossians and emphasized proper practice in the last portion of that letter. When we recognize that Christ is all sufficient and we are filled—or controlled—by His fullness, we will dramatically show this in our daily living.

Scriptural Test

I believe there is a foolproof scriptural test that can be applied to any teaching about Christianity. This test involves the following questions: Where does this belief place Jesus Christ? Is He only included in this belief, or is He the central focus of it?

Apply these questions concerning the centrality of Jesus

Christ to some of the beliefs you know. It is another way of asking the same question Jesus Christ asked the Pharisees: "What think ye of Christ?" (Matt. 22:42). We need to be sure we know the truth concerning Jesus Christ and that we believe it without reservation. Only then will we have the confidence expressed by the Apostle Paul: "I know whom I have believed, and am persuaded that he is able to keep that which I have committed unto him against that day" (II Tim. 1:12).

Paul didn't want to just know about Jesus Christ. Through faith in Christ for his salvation and for his daily living, Paul had grown to know Jesus Christ intimately. From experience, Paul knew what it was to rely on the indwelling Christ to give him the enablement he needed to face difficult situations. He had come to know experientially that Christ is all sufficient.

The false teachers in Colossae were not necessarily denying Jesus Christ, but they were dethroning Him from His rightful position. The false teachers of that day had not only robbed Christ of His rightful place of supremacy, but they had robbed the believers of their hope of complete victory, which is found only in Jesus Christ.

That the means of victory is through Jesus Christ is evident from what Paul said in his first letter to the Corinthians: "But thanks be to God, which giveth us the victory through our Lord Jesus Christ" (15:57). In his second letter to the Corinthians, Paul said, "Now thanks be unto God, which always causeth us to triumph in Christ, and maketh manifest the savour of his knowledge by us in every place" (2:14). No wonder Paul told the Philippians, "I can do all things through Christ which strengtheneth me" (Phil. 4:13).

Chapter 2

Paul's Opening Remarks to the Colossians

As Paul began his letter to the believers in Colossae, he wrote: "Paul, an apostle of Jesus Christ by the will of God, and Timotheus our brother, to the saints and faithful brethren in Christ which are at Colosse: Grace be unto you, and peace, from God our Father and the Lord Jesus Christ" (Col. 1:1,2).

The Human Author

In these introductory comments, Paul referred to himself, as the human author; to his associate in the ministry, Timothy; and to the recipients, the Colossians—whom he called "saints" and "brethren."

Paul was also known by the name "Saul" in his earlier days. "Saul" means "a great one," and "Paul" means "a little one." Saul was his Jewish name, and Paul was his Gentile name. After his conversion, the name commonly used was Paul. It is possible that he had both names from birth and simply chose to use the Gentile name to more closely associate himself with the Gentiles after his conversion. It is possible also that God gave him the name "Paul" at his conversion. In either case, the use of the name "Paul" emphasized his humility. Some people give the impression that they are almost too big for God, but this was not the case with Paul, and his humble spirit was portrayed in the name he chose to use.

Of various titles that Paul might have used in referring to himself, it is significant to notice that he used the title "apostle." This title especially emphasized his position as a chosen one who served as an ambassador of the Lord Jesus Christ. He was one appointed with special authority. His words were as binding as the One he represented.

Notice that Paul was not an apostle of some group of men; he was an apostle "of Jesus Christ" (Col. 1:1). The authority of the other apostles and of Paul was derived from God Himself, not from a human source. On one occasion, the Lord Jesus Christ told His disciples, "Ye have not chosen me, but I have chosen you, and ordained you, that ye should go and bring forth fruit, and that your fruit should remain: that whatsoever ye shall ask of the Father in my name, he may give it you" (John 15:16).

That Paul was an apostle of Jesus Christ "by the will of God" (Col. 1:1) suggests that God has a plan for every person's life. Paul had the consciousness that he directly represented Jesus Christ and that this position was according to the will of God. As one reads the New Testament letters that Paul wrote, he becomes aware of the fact that Paul had a serious sense of direction in all that he did. He was on a single course of pleasing God and doing His will. When opposition faced Paul on one occasion, he triumphantly announced, "None of these things move me, neither count I my life dear unto myself, so that I might finish my course with joy, and the ministry, which I have received of the Lord Jesus, to testify the gospel of the grace of God" (Acts 20:24).

God chooses and equips individuals according to His will so they might do special tasks as members of the Body of Christ. Occasionally I have had someone approach me for counsel about their entering a radio ministry. One of the things I am always concerned about is whether or not they are convinced God has called them to such a ministry. If God has truly called them, He will properly equip them to do the job. It is one thing to teach on the radio, but it is quite another to teach in a classroom situation. Although God has given me some measure of success in teaching on radio, I do not believe I would have made a good Bible teacher in the classroom. On the other hand, my son gains more fulfillment from the interaction of students in the classroom than from speaking before a microphone to a radio audience, although he does well in this also. Each one must decide where God has placed him and with what gift He has equipped him to accomplish the work of God.

His Associate

In writing to the Colossians, Paul introduced his associate in the ministry: "Timotheus our brother" (Col. 1:1). Paul was not hesitant to share the limelight with someone else. It is an indication of Paul's humility that he would quickly introduce his associate in such a significant and important letter as this one to the Colossians.

Paul's deep appreciation for Timothy is especially seen in Philippians 2:19-22: "But I trust in the Lord Jesus to send Timotheus shortly unto you, that I also may be of good comfort, when I know your state. For I have no man likeminded, who will naturally care for your state. For all seek their own, not the things which are Jesus Christ's. But ye know the proof of him, that, as a son with the father, he hath served with me in the gospel."

Many people today seem to serve from a motivation of selfishness. Although the specific questions are not always asked, sometimes it is apparent that believers are thinking of such questions as: What am I going to get out of this? How is my church going to benefit from this? If I cooperate in this venture, will it make me better known?

My wife and I frequently thank God for those He has called to join us on the staff at Back to the Bible Broadcast. Several of these people have been with us for many years, and they have evidenced unselfish attitudes, for they have not sought their own glory but the glory of God through this ministry. This kind of an attitude has made the working relationships positive ones over the years. It is a joy to work with those who have set their hearts and minds on finding God's will and doing it.

The Recipients

The Apostle Paul specifically directed his letter "to the saints and faithful brethren in Christ which are at Colosse" (Col. 1:2). The word "saints" means "consecrated ones" or "set apart ones." "Saints" is a title applied to all Christians without exception. Every person who has come face to face with his own sin and has trusted Jesus Christ as his personal Saviour is a "set apart one."

The Bible never uses the word "saint" to refer to the spiritual condition of an individual but only to the spiritual position of that person. It is a position of one who is born again by the Holy Spirit of God. It is not up to a man-made organization or the institutional church to declare a person a "saint." This occurs only when one has trusted Jesus Christ as his personal Saviour, and it happens to all believers without exception.

So one qualifies to be a saint by recognizing that he is a sinner, that Jesus Christ died for his sins and that by believing in Christ and turning from his sins he will have forgiveness of sins and eternal life. God then makes that person a saint; it is not the decision of a group of individuals.

Notice that Paul referred to the Colossians as "faithful brethren in Christ" (v. 2). The letter indicates they had been faithful both to God and to man. Whereas all believers are saints in God's sight, not all are "faithful brethren."

"Saints" speaks of position and relationship, whereas "faithful brethren" speaks of behavior. The Colossians were trustworthy, steadfast, unswerving in their devotion to God and man. So Paul was not only addressing those who were born again but also those who were honoring God in their daily lives as trustworthy, responsible believers.

How about you? If you have trusted Jesus Christ as your Saviour, you are a saint. But are you also faithful? Can God count on you? Can others count on you?

Grace and Peace

To that faithful, born-again group in Colossae, Paul said, "Grace be unto you, and peace, from God our Father and the Lord Jesus Christ" (Col. 1:2).

Grace is the source, and peace is the result. It is like cause and effect; the one who has experienced the grace of God is able also to experience the peace of God.

Paul's greeting combined the customs of the Greeks and the Hebrews. A common greeting for the Greeks was *charis,* meaning "grace." A common greeting of the Hebrews was *shalom,* meaning "peace."

There is a significant difference between the concepts involved in grace and mercy. Grace is God's giving us what we do *not* deserve—it is unmerited favor. Mercy is God's not giving us what we *do* deserve. It is by the grace of God that salvation is provided for us because we do not deserve it. On the other hand, it is by the mercy of God that He does not utterly condemn us because that is what we deserve.

Observe the source of the grace and peace: "From God our Father and the Lord Jesus Christ" (v. 2). In the expression "from God our Father," the word "God" invariably emphasizes strength. He is the Almighty God, *Elohim,* the Creator, the Sustainer, the One who has the ability to do anything He desires to do. But notice also that He is referred to as "Father." This word emphasizes the loving care for and interest in His children that God has for each of us.

The Father and Son are seen here in their unity because Paul also referred to the source of grace and peace as "the Lord Jesus Christ." It is only when we are rightly related to Jesus Christ that we experience both grace and peace from God.

Thanksgiving and Prayer

Having expressed this initial greeting, Paul told the Colossians, "We give thanks to God and the Father of our Lord Jesus Christ, praying always for you, since we heard of your faith in Christ Jesus, and of the love which ye have to all the saints" (Col. 1:3,4). From these two verses notice four special words: thanks, praying, faith and love.

Thanksgiving and prayer belong together like two wings of a bird. And both of these words are the expression of faith. Prayer is faith that asks. Thanksgiving is faith that takes. If you believe God will give it to you, you will ask Him for it. And thanksgiving shows that you are claiming it for your own.

People often pray, "Lord, when this comes about, we will thank You." But such an expression indicates the person is not really believing God will do it. If one believes God will do it, he can thank God right there and then. He can say, "Thank You, Lord, for the answer You will eventually give to this problem."

Almost everyone talks about faith because almost everyone has faith in something. But faith is only as good as its object. It is important to recognize that we are not saved from condemnation by having faith in faith. Paul commended the Colossians for their "faith in Christ Jesus" (v. 4).

So it is not sufficient to tell a person, "Just believe." The question is, Believe what? The message of the Gospel is not to believe in yourself, in church or in doctrine, but in the Lord Jesus Christ. This implies believing in all that Christ did for us when He died on the cross in our place. It recognizes that we are sinful human beings who deserve condemnation, or else it would never have been necessary for Christ to die. It means we recognize that Christ is our only hope because if we could have been saved by some other means, Christ would not have had to die (see Gal. 2:21). Having faith in Jesus Christ implies we have placed our confidence entirely in His finished work on the cross, recognizing that He forgives our sins and gives us eternal life. One can summarize saving faith as a commitment to Jesus Christ who is our life and Lord. Faith in Jesus Christ as our Lord is also necessary for growth in our Christian walk. We will see this in more detail as we study Colossians 2:6,7.

Because the Colossians had trusted in Christ, Paul was also able to give thanks "for the hope which is laid up for you in heaven, whereof ye heard before in the word of the truth of the gospel" (1:5). The Gospel, or good news, was that the Colossians could experience forgiveness of sin and come into possession of eternal life by trusting Jesus Christ as their personal Saviour. And this decision of faith gave them a confident hope in what was laid up for them in heaven.

Having referred to the Gospel, Paul went on to say, "Which is come unto you, as it is in all the world; and bringeth forth fruit, as it doth also in you, since the day ye heard of it, and knew the grace of God in truth" (v. 6).

Think of it! Although this was no more than 35 years after the death of Christ, Paul was able to speak of the Gospel as bearing fruit "in all the world." Although there were not as many people then as now, remember that then they had no airplanes, no radios, no television, no printing presses—no means of rapid transportation or of communication to the masses. Yet the believers of that generation were taking the Gospel to the then-known world. Traveling by foot, camel and horseback, the first-century Christians were earnestly spreading the Gospel.

What are we doing to spread the Gospel with all the means available to us? Although the population is much greater now, quick transportation and mass communication are at our disposal to reach a lost world. Let us renew our commitment to utilize the available methods to proclaim the Gospel of Jesus Christ to our generation.

Chapter 3

The Apostle's Sevenfold Prayer

Having communicated his greetings to the believers in Colossae, Paul explained what he had been praying for them. The apostle wrote: "For this cause we also, since the day we heard it, do not cease to pray for you, and to desire that ye might be filled with the knowledge of his will in all wisdom and spiritual understanding" (Col. 1:9).

Notice the reason for Paul's prayer as expressed by the words "for this cause" (v. 9). Paul referred back to what he had already said to the Colossians, in particular what he had heard about their faith in Christ and love to the saints (v. 4). Although Paul had never met the believers in Colossae, he was so moved by the reports of their faith in Christ and love toward the saints that he constantly poured out his heart in prayer for them. As he referred to what he had prayed for the Colossian believers, it is apparent that Paul was concerned for their continued spiritual growth and maturity.

Fully Know God's Will

The first petition Paul mentioned was "that ye might be filled with the knowledge of his will in all wisdom and spiritual understanding" (Col. 1:9). This first petition provides a foundation for all that follows.

Paul didn't want the Colossian believers just to be filled with knowledge, but it was to be the knowledge of God's will and was to be in all wisdom and spiritual understanding. This petition, then, is for the full knowledge of God's will and spiritual perception.

The word "filled" in its various forms is the key word in the Book of Colossians. It means "to be complete" or "to be filled full." We see this especially emphasized in Colossians 2:9,10: "For in him dwelleth all the fulness of the Godhead bodily.

And ye are complete in him, which is the head of all principality and power."

Referring to the fullness which is in Jesus Christ, John 1:16 says, "And of his fulness have all we received, and grace for grace."

In the New Testament, the word translated "fill" can also have the sense of "control." This is evident from the context of Ephesians 5:18: "Be not drunk with wine, wherein is excess; but be filled with the Spirit." The one who is drunk with wine is controlled by what he has drunk. In contrast to such a condition, the believer is to be controlled by the indwelling Holy Spirit. Since the Holy Spirit is a Person, it is not possible to get more of Him. The need of the believer is to submit himself to the complete control of the indwelling Holy Spirit, first by confessing any known sin, then by completely following the Holy Spirit's leadership.

As Paul prayed for the Colossians to be "filled with the knowledge of his will" (Col. 1:9), his desire was for them to be under the Spirit's control.

The Lord Jesus Christ Himself is the best example of One who was absolutely committed to doing the will of God in spite of the obstacles He faced. Although He did not have a sin nature and had never committed an individual sin, Jesus Christ faced an awful death on the cross to pay the penalty for the sins of all others. While yet in the Garden of Gethsemane, before going to the cross, Jesus prayed, "O my Father, if it be possible, let this cup pass from me: nevertheless not as I will, but as thou wilt" (Matt. 26:39). Even though Jesus did not desire to experience death on the cross, He was more than willing to do so because of His love for fallen mankind. Hebrews 12:2 says, "Who for the joy that was set before him endured the cross, despising the shame, and is set down at the right hand of the throne of God." What a wonderful God we have!

As Paul prayed for the believers in Colossae, he was concerned that they fully know the will of God. Paul prayed a similar prayer for the believers in Ephesus: "That the God of our Lord Jesus Christ, the Father of glory, may give unto you the spirit of wisdom and revelation in the knowledge of him" (Eph. 1:17).

The measure of the knowledge Paul petitioned for the

Colossians is seen from the words "filled with" (Col. 1:9). It is evident from the context that Paul desired for the believers in Colossae to have a practical knowledge of what is right and true in the sight of God. This knowledge specifically consisted of the knowledge of His will "in all wisdom and spiritual understanding."

Although the word Paul used for wisdom was the common word used in the first century, he used it in Colossians to refer to spiritual perception. Paul was referring to wisdom which originates with God alone. Such wisdom is especially emphasized in the Book of Proverbs, which states: "The fear of the Lord is the beginning of wisdom" (9:10). All true spiritual wisdom comes from God; it does not originate with fallen mankind. In fact, for the believer, Christ Himself is his wisdom: "But of him are ye in Christ Jesus, who of God is made unto us wisdom" (I Cor. 1:30).

Paul was especially concerned that the believers in Colossae might "be filled with the knowledge of his will in all . . . spiritual understanding" (Col. 1:9). The word "understanding" seems to emphasize the intelligent application of God-given wisdom. In a sense, it is similar to the contrast that is often made between knowledge and wisdom. Knowledge is an accumulation of facts, whereas wisdom is the proper application of those facts to a particular situation. Paul prayed that the Colossians might receive wisdom from God. He wanted them to apply what they knew to their own situations.

It is regrettable that many believers today have only a superficial knowledge of God. Such people become easy prey to various errors because they do not know how to apply their knowledge when they hear of a teaching that is new to them. Because of this lack, they are like "children, tossed to and fro, and carried about with every wind of doctrine" (Eph. 4:14).

This situation calls for consistent Bible study because one only grows in the knowledge of the will of God as he grows in his knowledge of the Word of God. We can be thankful that God has not only provided all we need for salvation but also all we need for godly living and discernment of His will (see II Pet. 1:3,4).

In chapters 1 and 2 of Colossians, wisdom and knowledge

are emphasized along with the understanding that Christ is all and in all. Jesus Christ is fully God (2:9), and He indwells each believer (1:27). Therefore, each believer is complete in Him (2:10). These are the truths that each believer needs to master for himself so they can be effectively applied to daily living. Knowledge of these truths and a wise application of them will produce a unity of faith among believers. We are to keep edifying each other "till we all come in the unity of the faith, and of the knowledge of the Son of God, unto a perfect man, unto the measure of the stature of the fulness of Christ" (Eph. 4:13). This is a lifelong process. Even the Apostle Paul did not consider himself to have reached the point where he could say, "I have arrived" (see Phil. 3:10-14).

Know How to Walk

Paul's second prayer for the Colossians was "that [they] might walk worthy of the Lord unto all pleasing" (Col. 1:10). Paul wanted them to know God's will, not just for information but also so they might know how to order their daily lives. Knowledge of the will of God is intended to lead to wise, practical living which will glorify God.

The word "walk" is frequently used in Scripture to describe the outward, or visible, expression of one's Christian life. It emphasizes progressing in conduct by taking one step at a time.

Occasionally, the Apostle Paul used the word "run" as he likened the Christian life to running a race (see I Cor. 9:24,26; Gal. 5:7), but the word translated walk is used much more frequently in describing the Christian life. Paul's constant prayer that the Colossian believers might "walk worthy of the Lord unto all pleasing" (Col. 1:10) indicated his intense desire that these believers' daily lives would honor the Lord. Of course, none can really be worthy of the Lord, but it is possible to walk in a worthy manner so that Christ is honored by one's daily life.

Do you live in such a way that attention is focused on Christ rather than on yourself? Is it apparent to other believers that you are pleasing the Lord by the way you live?

Many of the verses which follow in Colossians emphasize the greatness of the Lord Jesus Christ. He is described as being above all else, and yet He Himself is our life. What a humbling thought! These truths should motivate us to live in such a way that the world would stand in awe as they see what Jesus Christ can do, and is doing, not only *for* us but also *with* us.

Other New Testament portions emphasize the worthy manner in which we should live and thereby please the Lord. Ephesians 4:1 says, "I therefore, the prisoner of the Lord, beseech you that ye walk worthy of the vocation wherewith ye are called." Philippians 1:27 says, "Let your conversation [conduct] be as it becometh the gospel of Christ." Here the Apostle Paul referred to the same Gospel which he told the Romans is "the power of God unto salvation to every one that believeth" (Rom. 1:16). Such a Gospel changes one's entire life; therefore, he should walk in a worthy manner to glorify the Lord Jesus Christ who did so much in his behalf.

When we walk in a manner worthy of the Gospel, we will attract others to Christ rather than repel them. How sad it is to occasionally hear an unbeliever say, "If that person is a Christian, I do not want to be one."

As Paul prayed for the Colossians and their walk, or way of life, he did not pray that it might be pleasing to man but to God. In his letter to the Galatians, Paul said of himself, "For do I now persuade men, or God? or do I seek to please men? for if I yet pleased men, I should not be the servant of Christ" (1:10). Of course, when we live in a way that pleases God, many people will also be pleased by the way we live. But our focus of attention should be on pleasing God rather than people.

In Ephesians 6:6, Paul described how Christians should please their employers: "Not with eyeservice, as menpleasers; but as the servants of Christ, doing the will of God from the heart." This same emphasis is seen in Colossians 3:22: "Servants, obey in all things your masters according to the flesh; not with eyeservice, as menpleasers; but in singleness of heart, fearing God."

Living in a way that pleases God cannot be done in one's own strength. It is only by means of the indwelling Christ that the believer can exhibit the fruit of the Spirit and have a walk that pleases the Lord.

Although the believer seeks primarily to please God, not people, we must keep these truths in balance. We will not be successful in reaching others with the Gospel if we constantly displease them by our attitudes and actions. But above all, we must be true to God Himself in all that we do. As Paul sought to evangelize the lost, he was very careful not to unnecessarily offend those he was endeavoring to reach. Paul summed up this aspect of his life in this way: "Even as I please all men in all things, not seeking mine own profit, but the profit of many, that they may be saved" (I Cor. 10:33).

Paul endeavored to reach each person where he was and to establish a common bond with him. Although a Jew himself, Paul had been liberated from all of the ceremonial regulations of the Old Testament because he had found salvation in Jesus Christ as his Messiah. However, in seeking to win the Jews, he did not do those things that would be contrary to their conscience and ruin his opportunity to reach them for Christ. His manner of seeking to reach others with the Gospel is clearly spelled out in I Corinthians 9:19-23: "For though I be free from all men, yet have I made myself servant unto all, that I might gain the more. And unto the Jews I became as a Jew, that I might gain the Jews; to them that are under the law, as under the law, that I might gain them that are under the law; to them that are without law, as without law, (being not without law to God, but under the law to Christ,) that I might gain them that are without law. To the weak became I as weak, that I might gain the weak: I am made all things to all men, that I might by all means save some. And this I do for the gospel's sake, that I might be partaker thereof with you."

This passage has been commonly misunderstood. I believe Paul was emphasizing that he endeavored to establish a common bond with various individuals and not offend anyone in the process of winning them to Christ. I think when Paul was with the Jews, he emphasized his Jewish background; and when he was with the Gentiles, he emphasized that he was an apostle to the Gentiles.

In my own case, my background is Mennonite, and when I am with them, I do not mind letting them know that is my background. That helps them to realize that I understand them. On the other hand, if I am with Baptists, I do not mind letting them know that I graduated from a Baptist seminary. There are other examples of this principle, but I stress again that I see I Corinthians 9:19-23 as Paul's endeavor to establish a common bond with those to whom he was witnessing. Of course, Paul did not—and we must not—compromise truth in anything we say or do.

Some people interpret Paul's remarks in I Corinthians 9 as being compromise rather than establishing a common bond upon which a meaningful relationship can be based. For instance, I know of a radio station manager who once used this passage to justify why he permitted every kind of religious program on his station—he wanted to be "all things to all men" (v. 22). This person was twisting Paul's comments out of context. Everything done to please others must be subordinate to pleasing God. Only then can we be pleasing men for their good.

Bear Fruit and Increase in Knowledge

Paul's third petition on behalf of the Colossians was that they should be "fruitful in every good work" (Col. 1:10). There is an interesting parallel between verses 6 and 10. Paul used the same Greek words in referring to bearing fruit and increasing in knowledge in these verses. The parallel is better seen in another translation. In verse 6, Paul referred to the Gospel which "is constantly bearing fruit and increasing" (NASB). In verse 10 Paul referred to his desire for the believers in Colossae to be "bearing fruit in every good work and increasing in the knowledge of God" (NASB). As believers bear fruit and increase in the knowledge of God, the Gospel bears fruit and increases its effect in the world.

The Scriptures emphasize the importance of Christians' "being fruitful in every good work" (v. 10). The same truth is seen in Ephesians 2:10: "For we are his workmanship, created in Christ Jesus unto good works, which God hath before ordained that we should walk in them." Jesus Himself told believers, "Ye have not chosen me, but I have chosen you, and ordained you, that ye should go and bring forth fruit, and that your fruit should remain: that whatsoever ye shall ask of the Father in my name, he may give it you" (John 15:16). We bear fruit as we manifest the fruit of the Spirit (see Gal. 5:22,23) and as we reproduce ourselves by leading others to Christ.

Before He left this earth, Jesus said to His disciples, "Ye

shall receive power, after that the Holy Ghost is come upon you: and ye shall be witnesses unto me both in Jerusalem, and in all Judaea, and in Samaria, and unto the uttermost part of the earth" (Acts 1:8).

John 15:1-17 records the words of Christ concerning the bearing of fruit. "Every branch in me that beareth not fruit he taketh away: and every branch that beareth fruit, he purgeth it, that it may bring forth more fruit" (v. 2). Jesus also told His disciples, "Abide in me, and I in you. As the branch cannot bear fruit of itself, except it abide in the vine; no more can ye, except ye abide in me. I am the vine, ye are the branches: He that abideth in me, and I in him, the same bringeth forth much fruit: for without me ye can do nothing" (vv. 4,5).

The writer of the Book of Hebrews concluded his epistle with the benediction that God would "make you perfect in every good work to do his will, working in you that which is wellpleasing in his sight, through Jesus Christ; to whom be glory for ever and ever. Amen" (13:21).

Increasingly Comprehend God's Greatness

The fourth petition that Paul made for the Colossians was that they might be "increasing in (and by) the knowledge of God—with fuller, deeper and clearer insight, acquaintance and recognition" (Col. 1:10, Amplified).

Each of us who knows Jesus Christ as personal Saviour desperately needs to increase in our knowledge of God. For most of us, our concept of God is far too small. He has not only paid the penalty for our sin, but also He now indwells us to accomplish great and wonderful things in our lives. Let us grow in our comprehension of the greatness of Almighty God.

There are many biblical examples of new heights reached by those who obtained a greater comprehension of the greatness of God. Moses was one such person. He received excellent training in the house of Pharaoh for 40 years. There he gained much ability in governing, military procedure and organizing—abilities which he would draw on later as the leader of the Israelites. Although he gave himself wholeheartedly to God to lead the Israelites from Egypt, Moses did not really know the true greatness of God until

God took him aside for 40 years in the desert. At the age of 80, Moses was much different because of this private schooling than he had been at the age of 40.

Jonah is also an example. He had a small concept of God when he was told to go to Nineveh, for he thought he could run away from God. But after three days and three nights in "fish college," Jonah was more than willing to go to Nineveh. Why? Because he had a far greater concept of the greatness of God.

Peter boasted that he would follow Jesus anywhere in spite of what happened, but instead he wound up denying the Lord. After the crucifixion the Holy Spirit came upon Peter at Pentecost. Peter was then a different man because he had a greater concept of the greatness of Jesus Christ.

The Apostle Paul is another example. As he wrote to the Philippian believers toward the end of his life, Paul emphasized that his greatest desire was to know Christ better because he had not yet attained as he desired to.

The Colossians needed a greater comprehension of the greatness of God; so Paul prayed that they would be "increasing in the knowledge of God" (v. 10). God's greatness is later emphasized especially in verse 27: "To whom God would make known what is the riches of the glory of this mystery among the Gentiles; which is Christ in you, the hope of glory." Also 2:9,10 emphasizes his greatness: "For in him dwelleth all the fulness of the Godhead bodily. And ye are complete in him, which is the head of all principality and power."

Increasing in the knowledge of God involves a constant process of growth. It is not achieved by some sensational experience at a moment in time. Some people seem to think this is the case, but it is quite the opposite. Just as it took Moses 40 years in the desert to appreciate God's greatness, so it takes us time to understand God's working in our lives.

Paul knew that increasing in the knowledge of God takes time. He told the Philippians, "Brethren, I count not myself to have apprehended: but this one thing I do, forgetting those things which are behind, and reaching forth unto those things which are before, I press toward the mark for the prize of the high calling of God in Christ Jesus" (Phil. 3:13,14).

The Apostle John wrote: "Beloved, now are we the sons of God, and it doth not yet appear what we shall be: but we know that, when he shall appear, we shall be like him; for we shall see him as he is. And every man that hath this hope in him purifieth himself, even as he is pure" (I John 3:2,3).

Be Strengthened by His Power

Paul's fifth petition for the Colossians was that they might be "strengthened with all might, according to his glorious power" (Col. 1:11).

Paul prayed similarly for the Ephesians: "That he would grant you, according to the riches of his glory, to be strengthened with might by his Spirit in the inner man" (Eph. 3:16). Paul also exhorted the Ephesians: "Finally, my brethren, be strong in the Lord, and in the power of his might" (6:10). Notice, it is not our strength but His.

Paul's comments to the Colossians were building to a climax—the fact that Christ is supreme over everyone and everything. We have previously emphasized verses from the book which underscore this, and we will be looking at them in detail later. But Paul wanted no doubt left about the fact that Christ is all sufficient for the believer's needs. Paul wanted the Colossians—and all believers—to comprehend the superiority of Christ and to appropriate the supremacy of the indwelling Christ for daily living. Paul knew that such an understanding would produce strong believers. There is no room for weakness—that is why Paul first prayed that they might "be filled with the knowledge of his will in all wisdom and spiritual understanding" (Col. 1:9).

It is important for every believer to be strong *in* the Lord and *in* the power of His might. Paul also desired that the Ephesians might know "what is the exceeding greatness of his power to us-ward who believe, according to the working of his mighty power, which he wrought in Christ, when he raised him from the dead, and set him at his own right hand in the heavenly places" (Eph. 1:19,20). This is why Paul desired that the Ephesians "might be filled with all the fulness of God" (3:19). This led Paul to offer a benediction for the Ephesians: "Now unto him that is able to do exceeding abundantly above all that we ask or think, according to the power that worketh in us, unto him be glory in the church by

Christ Jesus throughout all ages, world without end. Amen" (vv. 20,21).

Notice especially the words "according to" in the phrase "according to the power that worketh in us" (v. 20). The power that is available to us is not according to our need, or even according to our capacity to absorb, but according to His ability to supply. Those key words "according to" appear in several other verses. Philippians 4:19 says, "But my God shall supply all your need according to his riches in glory by Christ Jesus." Ephesians 1:19 says, "What is the exceeding greatness of his power to us-ward who believe, according to the working of his mighty power."

It is significant that in these verses the words used are "according to" rather than "out of." If you are in desperate need and a millionaire gives you $100, he is giving to you "out of" his riches. However, if he hands you a signed check and tells you to fill it out for any amount you need, he is giving "according to" his riches.

God offers to give "according to," not "out of," His riches. We honor God as we allow Him to display His mighty power in our behalf.

Experience Joy Regardless of Circumstances

The sixth petition that Paul asked for the Colossians was that they might be strengthened "unto all patience and longsuffering with joyfulness" (Col. 1:11). *The Amplified Bible* renders this phrase: "[To exercise] every kind of endurance and patience (perseverance and forbearance) with joy."

Are you experiencing joy in the midst of your difficulties? Perhaps you say, "If you only knew what I am going through, you would understand why I have no joy." But Paul did not say that joy was possible only if the circumstances are of a special kind; he was praying that the Colossian believers would experience joy no matter how difficult the circumstances.

Again, each of us needs to ask himself, "How big is my God? Is He really able to give joy in the midst of extremely difficult circumstances? Is He really the all-sufficient One?" If you have questions like these, the Book of Colossians will be a very profitable study for you.

This sixth petition of Paul for the Colossians was that they might be strengthened "unto all patience and longsuffer-ing" (v. 11). Patience refers to things that happen around us. The original word translated "patience" is made up of two Greek words which literally mean "to remain under." Patience is the ability to remain under all kinds of trials and difficulties without becoming discouraged. The one who does not lose heart under such conditions indicates he or she has patience.

Long-suffering refers to a patience in regard to people. To have long-suffering is to have a quality whereby one is not easily provoked by those who do and say the wrong things concerning him. It is the ability not to fire up in anger against such persons but to be "forbearing one another in love" (Eph. 4:2).

Paul was not only praying for the Colossians to experience patience and long-suffering, but also he was praying that they might experience these qualities "with joyfulness" (Col. 1:11). A believer may endure with patience toward circum-stances and long-suffering toward people, but there may develop a certain gloominess or sourness of disposition. Per-haps you have noticed this. Sometimes you will ask a person, "How are you?" and he answers, "Well, I guess I'm getting along all right under the circumstances." Some believers are so "under the circumstances" they never seem to experience any joy in their Christian life.

Paul did not want the Colossian believers to be Christians with sour dispositions. He was convinced that it was possi-ble for them to be so strengthened with the glorious power of God that they could have joy along with their patience and long-suffering. And if Paul thought it was possible for the believers in Colossae, there is no reason to think joy is not possible for us today. But it cannot be manufactured by one's own strength; it comes only as we rely on the indwelling Christ and are "strengthened with all might, according to his glorious power" (v. 11).

When we appropriate what is available to us from the indwelling Christ, we will evidence the fruit of the Spirit in our lives, and joy is one of the manifestations of the fruit of the Spirit (Gal. 5:22). The Apostle Paul experienced a great deal of suffering himself, but he had joy in the midst of his suffering. He had asked the Lord three specific times to remove a serious problem from him, but Paul explained, "He said unto me, My grace is sufficient for thee: for my strength is made perfect in weakness. Most gladly therefore will I rather glory in my infirmities, that the power of Christ may rest upon me" (II Cor. 12:9).

The Book of Colossians was written for those who realize they do not have the strength in themselves to master their own situations. Those who realize their weakness can come to the all-sufficient Christ to receive help whenever needed.

The Lord Jesus Christ Himself victoriously displayed joy when facing extreme circumstances, and He now indwells us to enable us to do the same. This is why Hebrews 12:2 tells us, "Looking unto Jesus the author and finisher of our faith; who for the joy that was set before him endured the cross, despising the shame, and is set down at the right hand of the throne of God." The Lord Jesus Christ is our example, and none of us will ever have to go to the extreme He went. Although He was guilty of no sin, He took all the sins of the world upon Himself. In the midst of this mental anguish over the sin of the world, He could think of joy—the joy that was set before Him. It was the joy He could see on the other side of the cross after He had made salvation available. This joy was that He might have you and me with Him for all eternity because we have trusted in His finished work of redemption.

What does He see in you and me? In ourselves, nothing. But He sees what is possible as He works in our lives by providing redemption and all that we need to live a godly life. He is the all-sufficient Christ who is able to provide our every need.

Today we hear too much about resignation to do God's will and too little about delighting to do His will. Some believers give you the impression that they have resigned themselves to doing God's will because there is no other choice. How this must grieve the heart of God! Read the Scriptures, and notice the references that express joy in doing God's will. The psalmist said, "I delight to do thy will, O my God" (Ps. 40:8). Many other references in the Psalms express joy in doing the Lord's will. Psalm 40:8 is applied to the Lord Jesus Christ in Hebrews 10, even though the word "joy" is not used.

Hebrews 10:7 says, "Then said I, Lo, I come (in the volume of the book it is written of me,) to do thy will, O God." A similar concept is also expressed in verse 9.

Let us determine, by the grace of God, that we will not do His will *just* because we have to but because we want to. We will only come to this place as we recognize that He is the all-wise God who knows what is best for our lives. This realization will also help us to have patience with circumstances and to be long-suffering with people. James 5:11 says, "Behold, we count them happy which endure. Ye have heard of the patience of Job, and have seen the end of the Lord; that the Lord is very pitiful, and of tender mercy."

Patience in Job's case was not merely a resignation to the circumstances but a deliberate and persistent endurance of his extremely difficult trial. Notice God's pleasure in Job's joyful patience: "The Lord gave Job twice as much as he had before" (Job 42:10).

Give Thanks

Paul's seventh petition for the Colossians was that they might be "giving thanks unto the Father" (Col. 1:12). Paul went on to say about the Father: "Which hath made us meet to be partakers of the inheritance of the saints in light: who hath delivered us from the power of darkness, and hath translated us into the kingdom of his dear Son" (vv. 12,13).

Why do you think Paul was so concerned that the believers in Colossae would be giving thanks unto the Father? I believe it was because Paul recognized that the giving of thanks for the answers to petitions is a symbol, or proof, of faith.

Jesus said, "What things soever ye desire, when ye pray, believe that ye receive them, and ye shall have them" (Mark 11:24). If we really believe what the Lord said, we will thank Him for the answer even when we ask. In this same regard, Philippians 4:6 says, "Be careful for nothing; but in every thing by prayer and supplication with thanksgiving let your requests be made known unto God."

When we appropriate what God has for us, we will thank Him ahead of time for what He is going to accomplish in our lives. In this sense, the words "appropriating" and "thanksgiving" belong together. As we pray, let us not wait until we see answers to our prayers to thank God. Let us—by faith—thank Him for the answer at the very time we pray.

It is important for us to learn to take God at His word, or we will even question the forgiveness of our sins. For instance, I John 1:9 says, "If we confess our sins, he is faithful and just to forgive us our sins, and to cleanse us from all unrighteousness." I have heard many people say that they have confessed their sins to God, but they do not think they are forgiven because they don't *feel* forgiven. The real trouble is that such people do not really believe God, for He has said if we confess, He forgives. If this has been a problem with you, I suggest that when you confess any particular sin, you then say, "Thank You, Lord, for forgiving this particular sin." When we are intensely aware of the grievousness of our sins, we may not "feel" forgiven, but we need to take God at His word, for He forgives us on the basis of what Christ accomplished for us on the cross.

No wonder the Apostle Paul wanted the Colossians to develop the habit of "giving thanks unto the Father" (Col. 1:12). Note what the Father has done for us: "Which hath made us meet [qualified us] to be partakers of the inheritance of the saints in light" (v. 12).

Our common use of the word "inheritance" refers to what a person leaves at death to his or her heirs. An inheritance is what someone may expect in the future, but in the spiritual realm we possess the inheritance now. Therefore, we should thank God for it now.

In one sense we will receive an inheritance in the future which is reserved for us in heaven (see I Pet. 1:4,5), but we also have an inheritance here and now because God has qualified us "to be partakers . . . of the saints in light" (Col. 1:12). This is because of our standing in Christ, not because of our behavior. We have been made joint-heirs with Christ. However, it is important for us to appropriate these riches for ourselves.

For example, God had promised the land of Canaan to Abraham and his descendants. Yet in Joshua's time it was necessary for them to go into the land and personally take what had been given to them by God. God told Joshua, "Every place that the sole of your foot shall tread upon, that have I given unto you, as I said unto Moses" (Josh. 1:3). It had been given to the Israelites, but it was necessary for them to appropriate it for themselves. So also, blessings are ours in Christ Jesus, but we must appropriate them personally.

The Enemy of our souls will do everything he can to thwart our progress in entering victorious living as we appropriate our inheritance. But we should thank God for the riches that are ours in Christ Jesus and live daily on the basis of these divine riches.

Various Aspects of Salvation

Having indicated the seven petitions that he was constantly praying for the Colossians, Paul then referred to various aspects of salvation. One might call these God's provision of a sevenfold salvation. These aspects of salvation are emphasized in Colossians 1:12-22.

How could anyone ever turn away from, or try to add to, such a full, complete, divine and eternal salvation? Yet everywhere there are those who dare to turn from such a wonderful salvation and to substitute vain, human philosophy with all of its intellectual and ritualistic traditions.

Special blessings, which every Christian should be thankful for regarding salvation, are pointed out by Paul. First, the Father "hath made us meet [qualified us] to be partakers of the inheritance of the saints in light" (v. 12). We have already examined this truth in detail. Second, the Father "hath delivered us from the power of darkness" (v. 13). God has rescued us out of the control and dominion of darkness. This involves deliverance from the guilt and penalty of sin, but it includes much more than that.

Many Christians never seem to get beyond salvation. It is wonderful that they have trusted Christ as Saviour and have been delivered from the guilt and penalty of sin, but that is only the birth aspect of one's life with the Lord. What a shame it would be in the physical realm if one remained a baby. An infant is cute and nice to cuddle, but it is sad if a child does not grow beyond that point to maturity. Thus Christians should be thankful for their salvation, but they should go on to see all that Christ has for them in daily living and spiritual maturity.

Deliverance from the power of darkness has to do with the

way we live. Salvation makes it possible, but that is only the beginning. Ephesians 6:10-13 reveals the spiritual struggles of the daily life and how we are to be prepared for them. This passage states, "Finally, my brethren, be strong in the Lord, and in the power of his might. Put on the whole armour of God, that ye may be able to stand against the wiles of the devil. For we wrestle not against flesh and blood, but against principalities, against powers, against the rulers of the darkness of this world, against spiritual wickedness in high places. Wherefore take unto you the whole armour of God, that ye may be able to withstand in the evil day, and having done all, to stand."

God has made provision for us to stand against the powers of darkness. This is why Romans 13:12 says, "Let us therefore cast off the works of darkness, and let us put on the armour of light."

A parallel of salvation and spiritual deliverance from slavery to sin is seen in the experience of Israel in the Old Testament. When Israel was in Egypt, God rescued the Israelites from the judgment that came on the firstborn. He instructed them to kill a lamb and apply its blood to the doorposts of their dwelling (see Ex. 12). But if that would have been all that God did for the Israelites, they would have remained in Egyptian bondage.

The second aspect of God's deliverance was when He made it possible for them to cross the Red Sea and to be separated once and for all from the slavery and bondage of the Egyptians. God broke the power of Egypt. He did not destroy Egypt, but He broke its power over the Israelites. Many parallels exist here of the way God works in our lives today as believers.

The third aspect of the salvation which Paul emphasized to the Colossians was that God "hath translated us into the kingdom of his dear Son" (Col. 1:13).

The word rendered "translated" refers to being "transferred." It was used in Bible times to describe taking a population from one country to another, such as when the Israelites were taken captive by the Assyrians and Babylonians.

According to Colossians 1:13, God did not rescue us from bondage only to have us wander aimlessly. He moved us into the kingdom of His Son. Even as God delivered the Israelites from Egypt and took them into the Promised Land, so God rescues us from the realm of darkness and places us into the kingdom of His Son. In this sense, God brings us *out* in order that He might bring us *in*.

Notice especially the phrase "the kingdom of his dear Son" (Col. 1:13). A kingdom refers to a place of rule, and right now the believer is under the rulership of the Lord Jesus Christ. In this sense, every believer is in what can be referred to as a spiritual kingdom because he is under the dominion of Christ's rule.

A millennial kingdom will exist on earth when the Lord Jesus Christ Himself returns to earth to reign in a visible kingdom. It is yet future, but the spiritual kingdom exists now.

The spiritual kingdom, of which every believer is a part, is referred to often in the Scriptures. The following are some of the references. "For the kingdom of God is not meat and drink; but righteousness, and peace, and joy in the Holy Ghost" (Rom. 14:17). "Jesus answered and said unto him, Verily, verily, I say unto thee, Except a man be born again, he cannot see the kingdom of God" (John 3:3). "Except a man be born of water and of the Spirit, he cannot enter into the kingdom of God" (v. 5). "Flesh and blood cannot inherit the kingdom of God" (I Cor. 15:50). "That ye would walk worthy of God, who hath called you unto his kingdom and glory" (I Thess. 2:12).

Another significant observation can be drawn from Colossians 1:13,14: "Who hath delivered us from the power of darkness, and hath translated us into the kingdom of his dear Son: in whom we have redemption through his blood, even the forgiveness of sins." The verbs translated "delivered," "translated," "have" emphasize real action, not just potential action. We who know Christ as Saviour can say with certainty that God has delivered us, that He has translated us and that we have redemption.

For the believer the deliverance and translation are past acts, and redemption is a present possession. It is now important that we appropriate all that God has made available to us. For instance, Ephesians 1:3 says, "Blessed be the God and Father of our Lord Jesus Christ, who hath blessed us with all spiritual blessings in heavenly places in Christ."

But even though these blessings are ours in Christ, we must claim them in order to personally benefit from them.

As indicated previously, this truth has parallels to what God told Joshua. Although the land had been given to the Israelites, they were responsible to go in and actually take it for themselves (Josh. 1:3). The redemption which we have through the blood of Christ is ours to appropriate and enjoy now.

But there is even more. God's work through His Son in our behalf is all-inclusive. We have "redemption through his blood" (Col. 1:14). The special emphasis of redemption is deliverance from slavery which is obtained by the payment of a ransom.

To whom the ransom was paid is not stated, but certainly it was not paid to Satan, as some teach. It is clear, however, that by the death and resurrection of Jesus Christ, He met the holy demands of God's Law. Hebrews 9:22 states, "Almost all things are by the law purged with blood; and without shedding of blood is no remission [forgiveness]." Jesus Christ shed His blood and thereby paid the penalty for all sin. He completely fulfilled the Law by keeping it, and He paid sin's penalty by shedding His blood.

Our responsibility is to claim the benefits that Christ accomplished when He shed His blood for us, and we are to appropriate His resurrected life as our life. We need not be reticent in seeking help from Christ Himself, for Hebrews 10:19-23 says, "Having therefore, brethren, boldness to enter into the holiest by the blood of Jesus, by a new and living way, which he hath consecrated for us, through the veil, that is to say, his flesh; and having an high priest over the house of God; let us draw near with a true heart in full assurance of faith, having our hearts sprinkled from an evil conscience, and our bodies washed with pure water. Let us hold fast the profession of our faith without wavering; (for he is faithful that promised)."

In Colossians 1:14 the words "redemption" and "forgiveness" refer to the same truth; yet they emphasize different aspects. Redemption, as we have seen, emphasizes the aspect of setting free by paying a ransom. On the other hand, forgiveness emphasizes that our sins are crossed out as one would cancel a debt. God has not only delivered us and transferred us into another kingdom, but through the shed blood of Christ every debt against us has been cancelled so we cannot be enslaved again. Satan can never successfully bring the charge that there is another debt yet to pay. Christ has paid it all! He has delivered us and sent away our sins by paying the penalty for all sin—past, present and future.

Just as the country of Egypt still existed after the Israelites were delivered, a person still possesses the old nature after his spiritual deliverance. But just as God broke the power of the Egyptians over the Israelites, He has broken the power of the sin nature over the individual who has trusted Christ as Saviour. The removal of sin included sending away both the sin (the root) and the sins (the fruit). This applies to the past, present and future. Much more is involved than just the negative aspect of release from sin's bondage; there are also the positive elements of restoring, cleansing, justifying, sanctifying and glorifying.

What a wonderful assurance comes from knowing that one has been delivered from the power of darkness and that he has redemption and forgiveness of sins. And all of this is due to the grace of God, not to any merit of any individual.

The fourth aspect of salvation which Paul emphasized to the Colossians was that redemption centered in Jesus Christ: "In whom we have redemption" (v. 14). The phrase we have been considering, "even the forgiveness of sins" (v. 14), is the fifth aspect of Paul's sevenfold salvation.

Verse 21 portrays the sixth aspect in the statement "yet now hath he reconciled [you]." The seventh aspect is seen in verse 22: "To present you holy and unblameable and unreproveable in his sight." How beautiful it will be when we are transfigured in this way!

Chapter 4

The Supremacy of Christ

Having shared with the Colossians what he had been constantly praying for them, Paul then showed them the supremacy of Christ in every detail of life. Paul's ultimate aim was to cause the readers to realize that Christ is all they need and that their completeness and Christian experience is in the One who "is all, and in all" (Col. 3:11). Because the Lord Jesus Christ is supreme, He is all sufficient for every need. Nothing can be added to Him in whom all the fullness of the Godhead dwells bodily (2:9). Because the believer is related to the One who is supreme, the believer is "complete in him" (v. 10).

Supremacy in Creation

In emphasizing Christ's supremacy, Paul first spoke of Christ's supremacy in creation. Having said that the believers have redemption and forgiveness of sins through the shed blood of the Son of God, Paul mentioned concerning Him: "Who is the image of the invisible God, the firstborn of every creature: for by him were all things created, that are in heaven, and that are in earth, visible and invisible, whether they be thrones, or dominions, or principalities, or powers: all things were created by him, and for him: and he is before all things, and by him all things consist" (Col. 1:15-17).

Paul said that Jesus Christ "is the image of the invisible God" (v. 15). This states a truth concerning the deity of Christ. He is the exact likeness, or representation, of the invisible God. He is very God of very God; that is, He is one with the Father, and He is God Himself. So then he who sees the "image" sees the identical likeness of God.

Various Scripture passages tell of the essence and deity of Christ. John 1:18 says, "No man hath seen God at any time;

43

the only begotten Son, which is in the bosom of the Father, he hath declared him." Concerning this verse, *The Scofield Reference Bible* states, "The divine essence, God, in His own triune Person, no human being in the flesh has seen. But God, veiled in angelic form, and especially as incarnate in Jesus Christ, has been seen of men" (p. 1115).

Jesus said of Himself, "He that hath seen me hath seen the Father" (14:9). In His high-priestly prayer to the Father, Jesus said, "I have manifested thy name unto the men which thou gavest me" (17:6). *The Amplified Bible* translates this verse: "I have manifested Your name—I have revealed Your very Self, Your real Self—to the people whom You have given Me."

John 1:14 says, "The Word was made flesh, and dwelt among us, (and we beheld his glory, the glory as of the only begotten of the Father,) full of grace and truth."

As to the inner essence of Jesus Christ, He was—and is—God. But one cannot see inner essence. John 4:24 says, "God is a Spirit: and they that worship him must worship him in spirit and in truth." In the Incarnation, Jesus Christ took on a human body so that He might live among men and eventually die for their sins. Hebrews 1:3 says of Christ, "Who being the brightness of his glory, and the express image of his person, and upholding all things by the word of his power, when he had by himself purged our sins, sat down on the right hand of the Majesty on high." I have indicated that one cannot see the real essence of God, but some might think that Romans 1:20 contradicts my statement: "For the invisible things of him from the creation of the world are clearly seen, being understood by the things that are made, even his eternal power and Godhead; so that they are without excuse." Nature can reveal the existence and the power— even the wisdom—of God, but it cannot reveal the very essence of God. Only in Jesus Christ do we have the invisible God revealed to us.

Since no mere creature can reveal God, it is imperative that we understand the truth that Jesus Christ is God. Some today believe Jesus Christ is less than God. Some even say that the expression "Son of God" implies He is less than God. However, the Jews of Christ's day clearly understood that His claim to be the Son of God meant that He was making

Himself equal to God. John 5:18 says, "Therefore the Jews sought the more to kill him, because he not only had broken the sabbath, but said also that God was his Father, making himself equal with God."

Four significant observations can be made from Colossians 1:15-17. First, Christ existed prior to all creation. He is "the firstborn of every creature" (v. 15). From the original language of the New Testament, this phrase is literally "firstborn of all creation." The Greek word translated "firstborn" does not mean that He was the first one born; rather, it emphasizes priority and sovereignty. He existed before anything was ever created. This truth is obvious from verse 16: "For by him were all things created." He had to exist before all created things in order to create them. And because He is the Creator of all things, this implies sovereignty.

John 1:1-3 states, "In the beginning was the Word, and the Word was with God, and the Word was God. The same was in the beginning with God. All things were made by him; and without him was not any thing made that was made." Notice especially verse 3: "All things were made by him; and without him was not any thing made that was made." This directly connects with the truth presented in Colossians 1:15. The emphasis, then, of "firstborn" is one of rank and is not related to birth as we commonly think of it. Psalm 89:27 uses the word "firstborn" in referring to David's son, but it looks ahead to Christ: "I will make him my firstborn, higher than the kings of the earth."

Since Colossians 1:17 indicates that the Lord Jesus Christ existed before all created things, He Himself is uncreated, thus eternal. This verse says, "He is before all things, and by him all things consist." He is the eternal God; therefore, He is the Supreme Being.

The prepositions in verses 16 and 17 further reveal Christ's relationship to creation. Verse 16 says, "By him ... by him ... for him." Verse 17 also says, "By him." All things were not only created by Him but for Him, and it is by His power that they consist, or hold together.

Verse 16 especially emphasizes that Jesus Christ is the agent of all creation: "For by him were all things created, that are in heaven, and that are in earth, visible and invisible, whether they be thrones, or dominions, or principalities, or powers: all things were created by him, and for him."

Because Jesus Christ created all things He is sovereign over nature. The wind, the waves, even sickness, disease and death—all are ultimately subject to Him. When Jesus was on earth, He raised the dead (see John 11), and in the future He will raise the dead at the Rapture of the Church (see I Cor. 15:51-53; I Thess. 4:13-18).

Not only did Christ exist prior to all creation and was the agent of all creation, but He also created all things for His own pleasure: "All things were created by him, and for him" (Col. 1:16). All created things center in Him, depend on Him and serve Him. Since everything in creation exists for Him, then nothing that was created can be evil in itself.

Although our bodies now possess a sin nature which is evil, the body itself is not evil. The evil nature was not acquired until after Adam's fall.

Even Satan and his angels were first created as special servants of God (see Isa. 14:12-17; Ezek. 28:12-19). Lucifer, possibly the highest of the cherubim, fell because of his pride and was later known as Satan or the Devil. God is sovereign over him, as indicated in the first two chapters of the Book of Job.

A fourth point about Christ's relationship to creation is that He is the Sustainer of all creation: "He is before all things, and by him all things consist" (Col. 1:17).

The word translated "consist" actually means "hold together." Apart from Him, the universe would explode. The Lord Jesus Christ keeps it together in the form in which He created it. It is Christ who is "upholding all things by the word of his power" (Heb. 1:3). The Lord Jesus Christ is not only the firstborn, but He is also the Upholder of all of creation. Because He holds the universe together, there is an ordered system instead of chaos. Particles in our system are so minute they are still being discovered by man. And even though scientists sometimes know what happens, in many instances they do not know why it happens. Man has no complete answer apart from God's revelation that all things hold together by the power of Christ.

Supremacy Over the Church

In Colossians 1:18 Christ's supremacy as the Head of the Body, the Church, is revealed: "He is the head of the body, the church: who is the beginning, the firstborn from the dead; that in all things he might have the preeminence." The word "church" is used in verse 18 to refer to the Body of Christ, of which He is the Head. Of all of the various images used in the Bible to refer to the Church, the Body seems to be the most common. Romans 12:4,5 says, "For as we have many members in one body, and all members have not the same office: so we, being many, are one body in Christ, and every one members one of another."

Elsewhere we are told, "For as the body is one, and hath many members, and all the members of that one body, being many, are one body: so also is Christ. For by one Spirit are we all baptized into one body, whether we be Jews or Gentiles, whether we be bond or free; and have been all made to drink into one Spirit. For the body is not one member, but many" (I Cor. 12:12-14).

Verse 27 says, "Now ye are the body of Christ, and members in particular." There is no doubt that the physical body is used to portray how the Body of Christ is to function. Every person who has trusted Jesus Christ as the Saviour is a member of the Body of Christ and thus a member of the true, universal Church. When believers congregate together, they form local churches; but the Body of Christ refers only to the universal Church, composed of all true believers.

The Body of Christ, of which Christ is the Head, is also referred to in Ephesians. Particularly notice Ephesians 4:12, 15: "For the perfecting of the saints, for the work of the ministry, for the edifying of the body of Christ . . . but speaking the truth in love, may grow up into him in all things, which is the head, even Christ."

Since the true Church is referred to as the Body of Christ, I wish to stress how a person becomes a part of that Body. As indicated previously, the Body is composed of all those who have trusted Jesus Christ as personal Saviour. When an individual repents of his sins and believes in Jesus Christ as his Saviour, he then is placed into the Body of Christ by the Holy Spirit. This is the significance of I Corinthians 12:13:

"For by one Spirit are we all baptized into one body, whether we be Jews or Gentiles, whether we be bond or free; and have been all made to drink into one Spirit." This is the true baptism of the Holy Spirit—that act of the Holy Spirit by which He places a person into the Body of Christ at the time of salvation. Do not confuse the baptism of the Holy Spirit with what is being taught by some today. The indication of I Corinthians 12:13 is that this baptism is once and for all at the time a person becomes born again because he becomes a member of the Body of Christ forever.

Furthermore, this baptism is not something which takes place after salvation—it is not a post-conversion experience. When a person trusts Christ as his Saviour, the Holy Spirit takes up residence in his life at that moment and places him into the Body of Christ. That every believer is indwelt by the Holy Spirit from the moment of salvation is evident from I Corinthians 6:19,20, where Paul indicated that a believer's body is the temple of the Holy Spirit. Also, Romans 8:9 indicates the Holy Spirit indwells a person from the moment of salvation: "But ye are not in the flesh, but in the Spirit, if so be that the Spirit of God dwell in you. Now if any man have not the Spirit of Christ, he is none of his." So those who would say it is possible to become a believer without receiving the Holy Spirit at the time of salvation are teaching contrary to Romans 8:9.

In referring to the Church as the Body of Christ, we are referring to a spiritual organism, not an ecclesiastical organization. It is possible to be a member of this Church only by a personal relationship with Jesus Christ, having acknowledged one's sins and placed his trust in the finished work of Christ as his only hope of salvation.

As the physical body cannot function without its head, so the Body of Christ cannot function without Jesus Christ, the Head of the Body. The word "head" emphasizes source or origin as well as leadership and rulership. Thus, by trusting Jesus Christ as the Saviour and being baptized into the Body of Christ, we are united to the Head, who is the source of all life. As such, He is to be the leader and ruler of our lives.

As the head directs and controls all the activities of the human body, so Christ—the Head of the Church—directs and controls all of the activities of the Church, His spiritual Body.

Consider other Scripture passages which emphasize the headship of Christ over His Body. Ephesians 1:22,23 says, "And hath put all things under his feet, and gave him to be the head over all things to the church, which is his body, the fulness of him that filleth all in all."

The Apostle Paul used the relationship of the Church to Christ to instruct about a proper relationship of wives to their husbands. "Therefore as the church is subject unto Christ, so let the wives be to their own husbands in every thing" (5:24). In addition to teaching about the home, this verse emphasizes that the Church is to be subject to its Head, the Lord Jesus Christ.

In the first chapter we looked at the contrast between Ephesians and Colossians regarding Christ and the Church. Ephesians emphasizes the Body. Therefore, emphasis is placed on the unity of the members of the Body with the Head.

Colossians, on the other hand, emphasizes the Head of the Body, the Lord Jesus Christ. As the Head, He is presented as the source of all spiritual life, just as He is the source of all material life in the universe (see Col. 1:16,17).

Christ Himself is seen in Colossians as the guarantee of spiritual unity. Just as He holds all things together in the material universe, so spiritually He unifies the Church. He is the supreme authority over the Body. Because He bestows and controls all life, it is only reasonable that He would expect total loyalty, love and obedience from the Body.

But have you considered this? All nature obeys Him, but mankind—which is the capstone of His creation—does not obey Him. Relatively few acknowledge Jesus Christ as the true Head of the universe and fewer still as the Head of the spiritual Body. Too few repent of their sins and turn to Christ as their personal Saviour. May we who know Him as Saviour recognize His lordship over our lives, even as He is Lord of the universe.

Notice the threefold statement concerning Christ in Colossians 1:18: "He is the head, ... who is the beginning, the firstborn." We have already emphasized the first aspect which states, "He is the head of the body, the church." Let us now notice the second aspect: "Who is the beginning."

The logical question arises, Of what is He the beginning? I believe the context indicates it is referring to the Lord Jesus Christ's being the beginning of the Church. This statement must be taken with the third aspect emphasized about Christ in verse 18: He is "the firstborn from the dead."

Verses 15 and 18 both refer to Christ as the "firstborn." Verse 15 indicates He is the firstborn of "every creature" or, literally, all creation. Verse 18 indicates He is the firstborn from the dead.

The firstborn from the dead does not mean that Jesus Christ was the first one who rose from the dead. In the Old Testament, Elijah raised the widow's son (see I Kings 17:17-24). In the New Testament, Jesus raised the daughter of Jairus from the dead (see Mark 5:35-43), and He also raised Lazarus from the dead (see John 11:38-44). So again we have the significance of the Greek word that is translated "first-born." It does not mean "born first," as our English word seems to suggest. Rather, it stresses priority in rank. Of all those raised from the dead, the Lord Jesus Christ ranked first in importance.

Several statements are made in I Corinthians 15, which emphasize the importance of Christ's resurrection. Verses 17-23 state, "And if Christ be not raised, your faith is vain; ye are yet in your sins. Then they also which are fallen asleep in Christ are perished. If in this life only we have hope in Christ, we are of all men most miserable. But now is Christ risen from the dead, and become the firstfruits of them that slept. For since by man came death, by man came also the resurrection of the dead. For as in Adam all die, even so in Christ shall all be made alive. But every man in his own order: Christ the firstfruits; afterward they that are Christ's at his coming."

John 5:26 also emphasizes the importance of the resurrection. Jesus said, "For as the Father hath life in himself; so hath he given to the Son to have life in himself." Because Jesus Christ is God, He has existed from all eternity. He received life in a special way, however, not only when He entered the human race by taking upon Himself a human form but also later at the resurrection.

For mankind, spiritual life is determined by each person's relationship to Jesus Christ. The Bible says, "And this is the record, that God hath given to us eternal life, and this life is in his Son. He that hath the Son hath life; and he that hath not the Son of God hath not life" (I John 5:11,12).

It is not difficult to imagine, then, why Paul emphasized that Jesus Christ "is the beginning" (Col. 1:18). He is the beginning of everything, but the context of Colossians indicates it is referring to the beginning of the Church, which is His Body. And being "firstborn from the dead" (Col. 1:18), He became the source of all spiritual life and power to all who receive Him as personal Saviour.

Two elements are needed in order to regenerate an individual. There must be forgiveness of sin. However, if this were all that occurred, it would not be sufficient. This would be similar to removing a bullet from a dead man—the cause of death has been removed, but he is still dead. In addition to the forgiveness of sin, there must also be the giving of spiritual life. It is the good news, or the Gospel, that so dramatically changes a person's life. The Gospel enables a person to see his sinfulness and to see the need of believing in Christ as his Saviour. And it is the Gospel that changes the direction of his life from that point forward. This is why Paul could say, "I am not ashamed of the gospel of Christ: for it is the power of God unto salvation to every one that believeth; to the Jew first, and also to the Greek" (Rom. 1:16).

The power available through the Gospel is also seen in Ephesians 1:19,20: "What is the exceeding greatness of his power to us-ward who believe, according to the working of his mighty power, which he wrought in Christ, when he raised him from the dead, and set him at his own right hand in the heavenly places."

The position which believers have because of the power of the Gospel is seen in Ephesians 2:5: "Even when we were dead in sins, hath quickened us [made us alive] together with Christ, (by grace are ye saved)."

Without the Incarnation of the Lord Jesus Christ, we would be eternally doomed—separated from God forever.

The Incarnation is seen in John 1:14: "The Word was made flesh, and dwelt among us, (and we beheld his glory, the glory as of the only begotten of the Father,) full of grace and truth." What Christ accomplished by means of His Incarnation is seen in Hebrews 2:14,15: "Forasmuch then as the children are partakers of flesh and blood, he also himself likewise took part of the same; that through death he might destroy him that had the power of death, that is, the devil; and deliver them who through fear of death were all their lifetime subject to bondage."

Because Jesus Christ has done all of this for us, we can now boldly come to Him in full assurance of faith (see 10:19-23)! Christ has not only redeemed us, but He has also made it possible for us to come directly into His presence through prayer.

The Lord Jesus Christ is "the firstborn from the dead" (Col. 1:18) and "the beginning" of a new creation. The Bible says, "If any man be in Christ, he is a new creature [creation]: old things are passed away; behold, all things are become new" (II Cor. 5:17). Revelation 1:5 emphasizes the same truth: "And from Jesus Christ, who is the faithful witness, and the first begotten of the dead, and the prince of the kings of the earth. Unto him that loved us, and washed us from our sins in his own blood."

Thus, as firstborn of all creation (Col. 1:15), the Lord Jesus Christ imparts natural life. But as the firstborn from among the dead (v. 18), He has become the Redeemer and imparts spiritual life. This life is the new resurrection life of which He is the source, or origin. Because the life originates with Him, He is also the Ruler of those who have this life. By virtue of being the Head, Christ is thus designated to have all preeminence and all supremacy in everything, including His spiritual Body.

Supremacy in Everything

This brings us to the theme of this portion of the Book of Colossians—the supremacy of Christ. Colossians 1:18 says, "That in all things he might have the preeminence." The word translated "preeminence" means "to hold the first place." This reveals and magnifies the unique position that

Jesus Christ has today. This is why Paul emphasized in Colossians 3:11: "Christ is all, and in all."

Colossians 1:19 explains the reason for the previous great truths: "For it pleased the Father that in him should all fulness dwell." *The Amplified Bible* renders this verse: "For it has pleased [the Father] that all the divine fullness—the sum total of the divine perfection, powers and attributes— should dwell in Him permanently."

Because all now centers in the Lord Jesus Christ, we understand why Paul said, "Christ in you, the hope of glory" (v. 27). We also now better understand why Paul said, "For in him dwelleth all the fulness of the Godhead bodily. And ye are complete in him, which is the head of all principality and power" (2:9,10).

The question arises, What is meant by the word "fulness" mentioned in Colossians 1:19? Because it pleased the Father for all fullness to dwell in Christ, we can only understand the significance of that statement if we comprehend what is meant by fullness. From the context, the word simply refers to the sum total of the divine powers and attributes of God. This is especially seen in verse 18, which we have just been considering. In Christ dwells all the fullness of God as deity. Therefore, it is a heresy to make Christ less than God.

Look also at the word "dwell" in verse 19. The Greek word emphasizes a permanent dwelling, not just something that came upon Jesus for a moment of time. And of course, it is the same Jesus Christ who indwells each believer, as is seen from Paul's statement: "Christ in you, the hope of glory" (v. 27). Paul continued to build on this argument until he reached the climax of his statement in 2:9,10, which I con- sider to be the key verses of the entire book.

Supremacy in Reconciliation

The Apostle Paul has presented with undisputable proof the absolute supremacy of Christ in His deliverance of the saints (1:13,14), in the creation of the universe (vv. 15-17), in His headship of the Church, which is His Body (v. 18), and in His divine fullness (v. 19). Having emphasized those great truths, Paul then presented Christ in His work of reconciling fallen man. Borrowing a phrase from Hebrews 2:3, one could refer to Colossians 1:20-23 as "So Great Salvation." The full text of Hebrews 2:3 says, "How shall we escape, if we neglect so great salvation; which at the first began to be spoken by the Lord, and was confirmed unto us by them that heard him." The process of bringing about this great salvation is detailed in Colossians 1:20-23.

Verses 20 and 21 introduce the subject to us: "And, having made peace through the blood of his cross, by him to reconcile all things unto himself; by him, I say, whether they be things in earth, or things in heaven. And you, that were sometime alienated and enemies in your mind by wicked works, yet now hath he reconciled."

Meaning of Reconciliation

These verses describe the meaning of reconciliation—Christ's making peace between God and man. Man was alienated from God because of the fall of the human race into sin. The reconciliation of man to God is made effective through the shed blood of the Lord Jesus Christ, for "without shedding of blood is no remission" (Heb. 9:22).

Nothing in us motivated Jesus Christ to die for us. "God commendeth his love toward us, in that, while we were yet sinners, Christ died for us" (Rom. 5:8). Because He did this for us, notice what else we can expect Him to do: "Much more then, being now justified by his blood, we shall be saved from wrath through him. For if, when we were enemies, we were reconciled to God by the death of his Son, much more, being reconciled, we shall be saved by his life" (vv. 9,10).

The sinner is reconciled (thoroughly changed) by divine power from a state of hostility toward God to a loving trust and desire to fellowship with God. Romans 5:10 indicates we are reconciled to God by Christ's death, and we are saved by Christ's life. The power of His life within us is the power we need to live a victorious Christian life. The Christ who is before all things, above all things, Creator of all things, Sustainer of all things and the fullness of God is presented as absolutely sufficient (totally able) to effect the perfect reconciliation of man to God. Such an emphasis by the Apostle Paul left no room for the false teachers who were harassing the Colossians by teaching that Christ was not enough, that they had to approach God through intermediate angelic beings because Christ was too far removed from God to help them.

And there are a variety of things that are added today to what Christ has done. Some add the Law to believing in Christ, others add an adoration of Mary to believing in Christ. But only Jesus Christ has reconciled us to God, and any system that demands belief in something other than the finished work of Christ for salvation is presenting a salvation of works and not of faith; therefore, it is false.

Concerning reconciliation, please understand that God is not the One who is reconciled; rather, man is reconciled to God. Because of the shed blood of Jesus Christ, God was satisfied that sin had been properly judged, but His attitude toward sin never changed—it will always be the same.

God is pleased to have all things reconciled to Himself. The whole universe will eventually be restored to harmony with God. Romans 8:21-23 states, "Because the creature itself also shall be delivered from the bondage of corruption into the glorious liberty of the children of God. For we know that the whole creation groaneth and travaileth in pain together until now. And not only they, but ourselves also, which have the firstfruits of the Spirit, even we ourselves groan within ourselves, waiting for the adoption, to wit, the redemption of our body."

Colossians 1:20 says, "Having made peace through the blood of his cross, by him to reconcile all things unto himself; by him, I say, whether they be things in earth, or things in heaven." The words "all things" do not mean those who pass from this life rejecting Jesus Christ as their Saviour. Some teach that eventually all will be saved, but this is not what the Scriptures teach. Those who reject Jesus Christ as Saviour are already condemned. John 3:18 says, "He that believeth on him is not condemned: but he that believeth not is condemned already, because he hath not believed in the name of the only begotten Son of God."

The Great White Throne Judgment of Revelation 20:11-15 clearly reveals that those who pass from this life rejecting Jesus Christ as Saviour will be cast into the lake of fire forever. They will be resurrected from death and hades to stand before the Great White Throne Judgment and to be "cast into the lake of fire" (v. 15).

Process and Effects of Reconciliation

Colossians 1:22 reveals the far-reaching process of being reconciled to God by the blood of Jesus Christ. Paul explained that Christ had reconciled the Colossians "in the body of his flesh through death, to present you holy and unblameable and unreproveable in his sight." The extent of Christ's reconciliation is seen in what He will accomplish for believers—to present them "holy and unblameable and unreproveable."

The word "holy" involves both imputed holiness and personal holiness. Imputed holiness refers to a holiness which was placed on the person's account at the time of salvation. This holiness relates to his standing. Personal holiness involves our sharing Christ's life and holiness, which is wrought by His indwelling power. This holiness refers to his state, or his behavior.

Christ also desires to present the believer "unblameable" (v. 22). This refers to a faultlessness or being without blemish. In fact, the same word is translated "without blemish" in Ephesians 5:27: "That he might present it [the Church] to himself a glorious church, not having spot, or wrinkle, or any such thing; but that it should be holy and without blemish." This same word was used of the sacrificial lamb that was to be without blemish. The Scriptures state that our salvation was not purchased with corruptible things "but with the precious blood of Christ, as of a lamb without blemish and without spot" (I Pet. 1:19). So according to Colossians 1:22, Christ is going to present each believer "unblameable" in his sight.

Another glorious part of the effects of reconciliation is that Christ will also present the believer as "unreproveable in his sight" (v. 22). The Greek word translated "unreproveable" means "free from accusation." Think of it! No one will be able to accuse the believer in any way. We are sinners saved by grace! All of this is done "in his sight" or literally "before Him" (v. 22). These three key words in verse 22 basically cover the entire status of the believer. "Holy" speaks of entire consecration and is the opposite of being alienated from God. "Unblameable" is the absence of blame, or fault. "Unreproveable" reveals that no accusation is possible.

Another way to view these three words is that "holy" is inward, or internal; "unblameable" is outward, or external; "unreproveable" is upward, or eternal.

All of these wonderful truths should cause the believer to rejoice and praise God. On one occasion when the Apostle Paul's heart was so overwhelmed, he exclaimed, "What shall we then say to these things? If God be for us, who can be against us? He that spared not his own Son, but delivered him up for us all, how shall he not with him also freely give us all things? Who shall lay anything to the charge of God's elect? It is God that justifieth. Who is he that condemneth? It is Christ that died, yea rather, that is risen again, who is even at the right hand of God, who also maketh intercession for us" (Rom. 8:31-34).

Permanence of Reconciliation

Having told of the far-reaching effects of reconciliation that were possessed by the believers in Colossae, Paul told them, "If ye continue in the faith grounded and settled, and be not moved away from the hope of the gospel, which ye have heard, and which was preached to every creature which is under heaven; whereof I Paul am made a minister" (Col. 1:23).

This verse has presented difficulty to some because of the first word, "if." There are those who say that this indicates it was possible for the Colossians to lose their salvation and, therefore, not be presented holy, unblameable and unreproveable before Him.

One is helped in resolving this problem, however, when he realizes that in the original language of the New Testament this construction could have the meaning of either "if" or "since." Only the context can determine which way to translate it. Paul would have been aware that occasionally unbelievers would be reading his letter to the Colossians. If the word is translated "if," this could have been Paul's way of letting those unbelievers know these truths did not apply to them. On the other hand, if the word is translated "since," Paul would have been thinking only of the believers. I believe this latter meaning is the one Paul was using. From other Scriptures which Paul wrote, I believe it can be defended that Paul did not believe it was possible for one to lose his salvation. Therefore, I believe he was assuming the reality of their continuing in the faith and that the best way to communicate Paul's meaning to us is to translate the word "since" instead of "if."

I believe the Scriptures are clear that one is not saved by continuing in the faith; rather, he continues in the faith because he is saved. His continuing in the faith is not a means of salvation but a proof of salvation.

Paul was addressing himself to those who had been born again; so he was not referring to retaining or keeping one's salvation. But he was referring to the possession of their salvation as evidenced by their continuing in the faith. Even though the believer has ups and downs in the Christian life, his standing with God is not changed because of this. However, I am quick to point out that if there is no change of behavior, then I doubt that a person has ever been saved. No believer will be able to live a perfect life, but the evidence of his salvation will be a sensitivity to sin and a desire to please Christ in what he does. A victorious walk in this world is assured as we live by faith in Jesus Christ. Colossians 2:6 says, "As ye have therefore received Christ Jesus the Lord, so walk ye in him." We received Christ by faith; so we are to daily live by faith in Him.

Let us return to Colossians 1:23, remembering that the Greek language, as well as the context, indicates the possibility of translating the word "if" as "since," which is in full harmony with the whole of Scripture. Thus, the verse should read: "[Since] ye continue in the faith grounded and settled, and be not moved away from the hope of the gospel, which ye have heard, and which was preached to every creature which is under heaven; whereof I Paul am made a minister."

Verse 23 supplies the assurance of the fulfillment of verse 22. Those who have accepted redemption find themselves firmly fixed and grounded in Christ Jesus, thus rejoicing in the hope of the glory of God. First Corinthians 15:58 encourages all believers: "Therefore, my beloved brethren, be ye stedfast, unmoveable, always abounding in the work of the Lord, forasmuch as ye know that your labour is not in vain in the Lord."

Colossians 1:23 contains four statements about the believers in Colossae: (1) "[since] ye continue in the faith"; (2)

"grounded"; (3) "settled"; (4) "not moved away from the hope of the gospel."

Their continuing in the faith indicates they were persisting in, adhering to, abiding by, the faith. The fact that they were grounded refers to terminology commonly used of buildings. In I Corinthians 3:11-15, Paul used the analogy of building to talk about rewards for the believers who serve well—and a lack of rewards for those who do not. He said, "For other foundation can no man lay than that is laid, which is Jesus Christ" (v. 11).

The foundation of a building is extremely important if the building is to stand firm. I well remember, when I was a young man attending school, that a tall building was to be constructed in the city. However, in order to get deep enough to reach bedrock, they had to put pillars down 160 feet. It was imperative that they had a solid foundation. So, too, with the believer—Christ is the bedrock of his faith.

The fact that the Colossians were settled (Col. 1:23) speaks of the stability of the building. The more solid the foundation, the more settled is the superstructure.

The fact that the Colossian believers were "not moved away from the hope of the gospel" indicates they were progressing on to spiritual maturity. In this same regard, Colossians 2:6,7 says, "As ye have therefore received Christ Jesus the Lord, so walk ye in him: rooted and built up in him, and stablished in the faith, as ye have been taught, abounding therein with thanksgiving."

Although Paul was addressing his letter to true believers in Colossae, some had only professed to be recipients of the work of the grace of God. But they followed the Colossian heresy that Jesus Christ was not God. Paul was not addressing this group but only the true believers. However, it is a reminder to us that there are always those who would dilute the Gospel of the grace of Christ by adding something else to it. People who do this have merely a profession but not a true possession; that is, they have never placed their faith in Jesus Christ as their only hope, as the bedrock of their salvation. It is imperative that we who know Christ as Saviour be in the Word regularly so we will not only learn of Christ but will also be able to detect doctrinal errors more readily.

Ephesians 4:11-14 reveals that God has given gifted men

to the Church in order to ground and equip the saints for the work of the ministry. This is so "we henceforth be no more children, tossed to and fro, and carried about with every wind of doctrine, by the sleight of men, and cunning craftiness, whereby they lie in wait to deceive" (v. 14).

How is it with you spiritually? If you should pass from this world today, are you sure that you are a child of God and would immediately enter His presence? The Bible says, "Examine yourselves to see whether you are in the faith; test yourselves. Do you not realize that Christ Jesus is in you— unless, of course, you fail the test? And I trust that you will discover that we have not failed the test" (II Cor. 13:5,6, NIV).

For your assurance, I quote again I John 5:11,12: "This is the record, that God hath given to us eternal life, and this life is in his Son. He that hath the Son hath life; and he that hath not the Son of God hath not life." How is it with you? Have you recognized your sinfulness and seen Christ as your only hope because He alone has paid the penalty for your sin? If you have placed your faith in Him as your Saviour, then you have the Son, and whoever has the Son has eternal life. If you have not yet done this, please do so before it is eternally too late.

Chapter 5

Christ in You: The Hope of Glory

We come now to a section of Colossians that is special because it emphasizes what the believer possesses in Christ.

Rejoicing in Suffering

Paul told the Colossians, "Who now rejoice in my sufferings for you, and fill up that which is behind of the afflictions of Christ in my flesh for his body's sake, which is the church: whereof I am made a minister, according to the dispensation of God which is given to me for you, to fulfil the word of God" (Col. 1:24,25).

At first glance, one may be uncertain about who is doing the rejoicing in verse 24. However, notice that verse 23 ended with Paul's reference to his own relationship to the Gospel: "Whereof I Paul am made a minister." He then continued in reference to himself by saying, "Who now rejoice in my sufferings for you" (v. 24).

Paul was in prison in Rome at the time he wrote Colossians, but instead of being ashamed and discouraged by his suffering, he rejoiced in it. Although he had never personally seen the Colossians (see 2:1), he considered his suffering to be in their behalf. Perhaps this is because Paul distinctly considered his sufferings to be for the cause of the Gospel and, therefore, his sufferings would benefit all believers.

Paul experienced an enormous amount of suffering for the cause of Christ. In writing to the Corinthians, he listed some of these sufferings. I believe it is important to consider all that Paul went through, because most of us go through so little suffering for the Gospel today. However, in some places in the world believers still experience intense suffering—and even death—for their stand for Christ.

Paul told the Corinthians, "Are they ministers of Christ?

(I speak as a fool) I am more; in labours more abundant, in stripes above measure, in prisons more frequent, in deaths oft. Of the Jews five times received I forty stripes save one. Thrice was I beaten with rods, once was I stoned, thrice I suffered shipwreck, a night and a day I have been in the deep; in journeyings often, in perils of waters, in perils of robbers, in perils by mine own countrymen, in perils by the heathen, in perils in the city, in perils in the wilderness, in perils in the sea, in perils among false brethren; in weariness and painfulness, in watchings often, in hunger and thirst, in fastings often, in cold and nakedness. Beside those things that are without, that which cometh upon me daily, the care of all the churches. Who is weak, and I am not weak? who is offended, and I burn not? If I must needs glory, I will glory of the things which concern mine infirmities" (II Cor. 11:23-30).

Paul was so humbled by the grace of God which provided his salvation that he did not consider it possible to suffer too much for the cause of Christ. That is why he said in Philippians 3:10, "That I may know him, and the power of his resurrection, and the fellowship of his sufferings, being made conformable unto his death." Notice especially his words "the fellowship of his sufferings." Paul desired to experience the power of the resurrection life which Christ has made available to every believer. And because Christ suffered to pay the penalty for his salvation, Paul considered it special that he could suffer for the cause of Christ so others might hear the message of salvation.

Peter also had much to say about suffering. He wrote: "Beloved, think it not strange concerning the fiery trial which is to try you, as though some strange thing happened unto you: but rejoice, inasmuch as ye are partakers of Christ's sufferings; that, when his glory shall be revealed, ye may be glad also with exceeding joy. If ye be reproached for the name of Christ, happy are ye; for the spirit of glory and of God resteth upon you: on their part he is evil spoken of, but on your part he is glorified" (I Pet. 4:12-14).

Peter added, "Yet if any man suffer as a Christian, let him not be ashamed; but let him glorify God on this behalf" (v. 16).

Although those who are suffering may have the tendency to think God is unfair, Peter encouraged them: "Wherefore let them that suffer according to the will of God commit the keeping of their souls to him in well doing, as unto a faithful Creator" (v. 19).

The attitude of the believers of the early church toward suffering is seen from the reaction of the apostles. On one occasion they were brought before the Jewish Sanhedrin, beaten and commanded not to speak in the name of Jesus. But the apostles departed, "rejoicing that they were counted worthy to suffer shame for his name. And daily in the temple, and in every house, they ceased not to teach and preach Jesus Christ" (Acts 5:41,42).

There is a reward for those who suffer for the cause of Christ. Jesus said, "Blessed are ye, when men shall revile you, and persecute you, and shall say all manner of evil against you falsely, for my sake. Rejoice, and be exceeding glad: for great is your reward in heaven: for so persecuted they the prophets which were before you" (Matt. 5:11,12). The same truth is emphasized in II Timothy 2:12: "If we suffer, we shall also reign with him."

The sufferings which Paul spoke of concerning the Colossians had nothing to do, of course, with suffering for their sin. Jesus Christ Himself paid the full penalty for sin. Paul saw himself only as one who was fortunate to have experienced the grace of God, and he was willing to suffer anything necessary to get the message of salvation out to others.

Responsibility to Others

Having mentioned Christ's Body, the Church (Col. 1:24), Paul said, "Whereof I am made a minister, according to the dispensation of God which is given to me for you, to fulfil the word of God" (v. 25).

Although today it is common to think of the word "minister" in a professional sense, the word simply means "servant." Paul saw himself as a servant who was responsible to take the message to others. This responsibility is seen in his words "according to the dispensation of God which is given to me for you."

The word translated "dispensation" means "stewardship." It is made up of two Greek words which are joined together, which literally mean "the law of the house." God had given responsibility to the Apostle Paul concerning the Church, and Paul wanted to be a faithful servant in carrying out that responsibility. No doubt that is why he was rejoicing for his sufferings in behalf of the Colossians; he was carrying out his faithful responsibility to the Gospel in their behalf.

Having mentioned "the dispensation of God," Paul further explained: "Even the mystery which hath been hid from ages and from generations, but now is made manifest to his saints: to whom God would make known what is the riches of the glory of this mystery among the Gentiles; which is Christ in you, the hope of glory" (vv. 26,27).

The "mystery" in the scriptural sense refers to something that had not been previously revealed but was now made known. When something is spoken of as a mystery in the New Testament, it is particularly emphasizing that it was not known in the Old Testament. But what specific truth did Paul indicate was not known previously?

Some think that the mystery was that Gentiles would be saved. However, that truth is not new to the New Testament. When God first called Abraham, He said, "In thee shall all families of the earth be blessed" (Gen. 12:3). Isaiah 53, which predicts the suffering of the Messiah, clearly states: "The Lord hath laid on him the iniquity of us all" (v. 6).

So it was no mystery that Gentiles would be saved, although many Jews in Paul's time resisted taking the message to the Gentiles. In fact, on more than one occasion Paul got into difficulty with the Jews when they discovered he was concerned about ministering to the Gentiles.

The mystery to which Paul referred in Colossians 1 is that the Jew and Gentile would be united in one spiritual Body and both indwelt by Christ Himself.

In his letter to the Ephesians, Paul emphasized the new truth that Jews and Gentiles would be in the same spiritual Body. Paul said, "Wherefore remember, that ye being in time past Gentiles in the flesh, who are called Uncircumcision by that which is called the Circumcision in the flesh made by hands; that at that time ye were without Christ, being aliens from the commonwealth of Israel, and strangers from the covenants of promise, having no hope, and without God in the world: but now in Christ Jesus ye who sometimes were far off are made nigh by the blood of Christ. For he is our peace, who hath made both one, and hath broken down the middle wall of partition between us" (2:11-14).

Any person who trusts Jesus Christ as Saviour during the present age becomes a member of the Church, the Body of Christ. Although a person is a Jew or Gentile according to the flesh, spiritually the believer in Christ loses national distinctions as a member of the Body of Christ. After the Church is raptured from the earth (see I Cor. 15:51-53; I Thess. 4:13-18), God will then again work distinctly with the nation of Israel during the Tribulation.

During Old Testament times it was necessary for the Gentiles to become Jewish proselytes in order to share the blessing of Israel. That is not necessary anymore because the "middle wall of partition" (Eph. 2:14) has been broken down. Jew and Gentile share equally in the spiritual blessings of the same Body. Gentile believers share the hope of supreme glory together with believing Jews. All the fullness of the Father dwells in Christ (Col. 1:19), and both Jew and Gentile are "complete in him" (2:10).

Romans 8:32 says, "He that spared not his own Son, but delivered him up for us all, how shall he not with him also freely give us all things?" This applies to Jews and Gentiles alike. All things are theirs as they are properly related to Jesus Christ. Christianity is more than a set of rules or ethics or morals or even doctrines—it is a relationship with a Person, the Lord Jesus Christ.

Concerning Christ, the message and the messenger cannot be separated. The Lord Jesus Christ not only speaks the truth, but He also implements it in our lives. Christianity and Christ are inseparable; one cannot exist without the other. Although there is a system of truth in Christianity, the believer must be constantly aware that he needs to focus his attention on the Person of the Lord Jesus.

Indwelling Christ

Colossians 1:27 says, "The riches of the glory of this mystery among the Gentiles; which is Christ in you, the hope of glory." This is a truth that was unknown in Old Testament times—that God Himself would indwell every believer. This was not true during Old Testament times, neither will it be true after the Church Age. Only during the Church Age—

from the birth of the Church at Pentecost (see Acts 2) until the Church is raptured from the earth (see I Thess. 4)—is it true that Christ indwells every believer.

That Christ indwells the believer is taught in many New Testament passages, such as Galatians 2:20: "I am crucified with Christ: nevertheless I live; yet not I, but Christ liveth in me: and the life which I now live in the flesh I live by the faith of the Son of God, who loved me, and gave himself for me."

Although Christ indwells every believer, as the believer matures, Christ is formed in him. Paul said to the Galatians, "My little children, of whom I travail in birth again until Christ be formed in you" (4:19). Christ is formed in the believer as the believer takes on more of the characteristics of Christ. Ephesians 4:24 says it this way: "That ye put on the new man, which after God is created in righteousness and true holiness."

The indwelling Christ is the believer's "hope of glory" (Col. 1:27). Since the believer is identified with Christ, having been made one with Him, Christ's glorified humanity in heaven is the believer's guarantee that he also will be glorified and eventually enter heaven. The Apostle John wrote: "Beloved, now are we the sons of God, and it doth not yet appear what we shall be: but we know that, when he shall appear, we shall be like him; for we shall see him as he is" (I John 3:2).

In the expression "Christ in you" (Col. 1:27) the words "in you" are very important. For those of us who know Christ as Saviour, He is not only our life, but He is also the life *in* us.

On the surface, the emphasis of "Christ in you" may not seem so important. But when we grasp the significance of this great truth, our thinking about Christ and ourselves will be changed and even our prayer life will be changed. I well remember when I was a young preacher and my father had grasped the glorious truth of "Christ in you." Those were good words to me, but I did not see the importance in them that my father did. But one of the red-letter days of my life was when God opened my inner eyes and ears to understand what it really is to be in Christ and to have Him in me. I then experienced a change in my outlook on life in general and on my prayer life in particular. I experienced a new insight and a new understanding of what it means to be able to say, "I live; yet not I, but Christ liveth in me" (Gal. 2:20).

The Lord Jesus Christ, who walked on this earth and who is now at the Father's right hand, must not only be a leader or teacher to us. It is not enough that He came, lived, died and rose again; He must be personally received as Saviour, at which time He will take up personal residence in our heart. And as we study the Scriptures to learn more about Him and apply the truths to our life, He will be formed in us.

An intellectual acceptance of the facts of Christ's Person and work is not sufficient for what we need and want. We certainly need to know those facts, but we must go beyond those facts to place our faith in Him as Saviour and to daily experience His living power in us. This is the thrust of the Book of Colossians, and that is why I think it is so important.

Many questions arise, such as: How can we be sure of life to come? How do we know we will have life eternally? Although there are many details that can be given in answering these questions, in the final analysis the answer is "Christ in you, the hope of glory" (Col. 1:27). Christ is eternal life.

Jesus Christ is God, and although He took upon Himself a human form to live among men and to die on the cross, He lives eternally. And it is this eternal life that indwells each one who knows Jesus Christ as Saviour. He is our eternal life. That is why I John 5:12 can say, "He that hath the Son hath life." And Jesus has assured us: "I will never leave thee, nor forsake thee" (Heb. 13:5).

So Christ put away our sin by His death, and our acceptance of the now glorified, risen Christ is our life. As Romans 5:10 says, "For if, when we were enemies, we were reconciled to God by the death of his Son, much more, being reconciled, we shall be saved by his life." We will be glorified because He is glorified, and we are united to Him. He is the all-sufficient Christ.

Preaching

Concerning the indwelling Christ, Paul said, "Whom we preach, warning every man, and teaching every man in all wisdom; that we may present every man perfect in Christ Jesus" (Col. 1:28). Notice four important words in this verse: preach, warning, teaching, present.

The word translated "preach" was a common word for "announce." Wherever Paul went, he announced the good news, or the Gospel, so that others would have an opportunity to hear of the salvation of grace through faith in Christ. What a privilege and an awesome responsibility it is to proclaim the message of forgiveness to fallen man!

As we consider the importance of the Gospel, we become aware that we are responsible to deliver the message of God to people, not just preach sermons. Years ago I remember hearing G. Christian Weiss say, "God never sent me to preach sermons; He sent me to deliver His message." I have never forgotten that statement, for it has burned deeply into my own life. As a result, I spend much time considering what the message of God is so that, as I speak, I might deliver it with urgency and not just pass on information.

Teaching

Let us next consider the word "teaching" in Colossians 1:28. Many wonder about the differences between preaching and teaching. Although many distinctions could be drawn between these two words, we will look at some of the more common ones. Preaching is proclaiming, whereas teaching is explaining. Preaching emphasizes the what, whereas teaching emphasizes the why. Preaching sets forth the facts, whereas teaching explains the relationship of the facts to each other. Perhaps it can also be said that the goal of preaching is persuasion, whereas the goal of teaching is understanding. These words overlap in their meaning; so it is not always possible to make sharp distinctions between the two.

Teaching should not just share information alone. When we're handling spiritual truths, we should desire to teach in such a way that people will understand and translate those truths into Christian living. On my 75th birthday, I received many cards and letters acknowledging appreciation for the Back to the Bible ministry. One, which I received from Steven Olford, especially encouraged me because of a statement he made: "There is Bible teaching that ends with Bible teaching, and there is Bible teaching that issues in changed living." He went on to say that he had found the Back to the Bible ministry to be Bible teaching that issued in changed living. This is a good reminder that whenever we preach or teach the Word of God, we should desire to see changed lives as a result of the message we give.

Warning

Let us now consider Paul's statement about "warning every man" (Col. 1:28).

Many in Colossae needed to be warned because false teaching was rampant. Warning can be done in two ways— positively by teaching the truth and negatively by confronting those teaching error.

The word translated "warning" in Colossians 1:28 means "admonish." Of the eight times this word appears in the New Testament, the King James Version translates it "warn" or "warning" four times and "admonish" or "admonishing" four times. The word refers to putting something into the mind which serves to admonish, or warn. When Paul gave his farewell to the Ephesians, he referred to his faithfulness in warning others. Acts 20:18-20 records Paul's words to the elders of the church of Ephesus: "And when they were come to him, he said unto them, Ye know, from the first day that I came into Asia, after what manner I have been with you at all seasons, serving the Lord with all humility of mind, and with many tears, and temptations, which befell me by the lying in wait of the Jews: and how I kept back nothing that was profitable unto you, but have shewed you, and have taught you publickly, and from house to house."

Paul was so confident of the effectiveness of the warning he had done that he was able to say, "Wherefore I take you to record this day, that I am pure from the blood of all men. For I have not shunned to declare unto you all the council of God" (vv. 26,27). Paul explained to the elders that opposition would arise from outside the church and from within. Paul urged, "Therefore watch, and remember, that by the space of three years I ceased not to warn every one night and day with tears" (v. 31). The Greek word translated "warn" in this verse is the same one translated "warning" in Colossians 1:28.

In the last recorded letter we have from the pen of the Apostle Paul, he told Timothy, "Preach the word; be instant in season, out of season; reprove, rebuke, exhort with all longsuffering and doctrine. For the time will come when they will not endure sound doctrine; but after their own lusts shall they heap to themselves teachers, having itching ears; and they shall turn away their ears from the truth, and shall be turned unto fables. But watch thou in all things, endure afflictions, do the work of an evangelist, make full proof of thy ministry" (II Tim. 4:2-5).

One of the most effective ways to warn others is to let them know how God has dealt with disobedient people in the past. As Paul wrote to the Corinthians, he warned them by telling how God had dealt with the Israelites during Old Testament times. Paul said, "Now all these things happened unto them for ensamples [examples]: and they are written for our admonition, upon whom the ends of the world are come" (I Cor. 10:11). The word translated "admonition" in this verse is the same basic word that is translated "warning" in Colossians 1:28.

Notice from Colossians 1:28 that Paul was warning and teaching every person "in all wisdom." Knowledge is the accumulation of facts, and wisdom is the proper use of those facts. Unless one properly uses knowledge, it will not be translated into changed living. Paul used the information he knew to warn and instruct every person so that the unsaved would respond to the Gospel and the saved would claim Christ's power for daily living.

The Lord Jesus Christ Himself is the embodiment of wisdom. Paul told believers, "But of him are ye in Christ Jesus, who of God is made unto us wisdom" (I Cor. 1:30). As believers, let us study the Word and learn more about Jesus Christ; then we can share our wisdom with others so they will be warned and instructed.

Observe the purpose of Paul's preaching, warning and teaching: "That we may present every man perfect in Christ Jesus" (Col. 1:28). The word "perfect" in this verse has no reference to sinless perfection. Much doctrinal confusion has occurred because the Greek word found in Colossians 1:28

has been translated "perfect." The Greek word does not mean perfection as we understand it; instead, it refers to that which is complete or mature. Paul did not want believers to be immature or to have undeveloped characters; he desired to see well-developed character and maturity in believers. One of the best Bible passages which shows how to be changed from an immature believer to a mature one is Hebrews 5:12-14: "For when for the time ye ought to be teachers, ye have need that one teach you again which be the first principles of the oracles of God; and are become such as have need of milk, and not of strong meat. For every one that useth milk is unskilful in the word of righteousness: for he is a babe. But strong meat belongeth to them that are of full age, even those who by reason of use have their senses exercised to discern both good and evil." We become spiritually strong as we take what we know and apply it to daily living. This exercises our sense of discernment, and we mature.

This is why Hebrews 6:1 says, "Therefore leaving the principles of the doctrine of Christ, let us go on unto perfection [maturity]."

Just as Christ is the source of our life, so Christ is also the source of our maturity. This is why Colossians 2:6 says, "As ye have therefore received Christ Jesus the Lord, so walk ye in him." The Christian life begins with Christ in us and continues with our being in Christ.

Colossians 1 concludes with Paul's words: "Whereunto I also labour, striving according to his working, which worketh in me mightily" (v. 29). Another translation says, "And for this purpose also I labor, striving according to His power, which mightily works within me" (NASB).

This passage reminds me of Paul's words in Philippians 2:12,13: "Wherefore, my beloved, as ye have always obeyed, not as in my presence only, but now much more in my absence, work out your own salvation with fear and trembling. For it is God which worketh in you both to will and to do of his good pleasure."

Paul was striving "according to" God's power, which was mightily working in him (Col. 1:29). This indicates that the work we are able to do is in proportion to the work God does in us. And He can only do in us what we allow Him to do. No wonder Paul wrote: "Be strong in the Lord, and in the power of his might" (Eph. 6:10). Jesus Christ is the life and strength in us. It is not just that we draw strength from Him; He is our strength.

Chapter 6

Complete in Christ

In Colossians 1 we saw an emphasis on the supremacy of Christ in all areas. In Colossians 2 the focus is on the incarnate Christ and the fact that we are complete in Him. As we recognize that Jesus Christ is fully God and that He indwells us, we will realize we have everything we need not only for redemption but also for daily living. This is what Peter stressed in II Peter 1:3: "According as his divine power hath given unto us all things that pertain unto life and godliness, through the knowledge of him that hath called us to glory and virtue."

Jesus Christ is everything we need for eternal life and our daily walk. Man-made methods or man-made rules can add nothing to what Christ has already accomplished for the believer.

Paul told the Colossians: "For I would that ye knew what great conflict I have for you, and for them at Laodicea, and for as many as have not seen my face in the flesh; that their hearts might be comforted, being knit together in love, and unto all riches of the full assurance of understanding, to the acknowledgement of the mystery of God, and of the Father, and of Christ; in whom are hid all the treasures of wisdom and knowledge" (Col. 2:1-3).

Complete Salvation

Paul expressed his deep concern for those living in Colossae and Laodicea because he realized false teachers had invaded their midst and were using enticing words and fair speech to mislead the people. We need to pay particular attention to this portion because we have the same situation today. Many claim to know Christ as Saviour but are presenting a message that takes the focus of attention from

Christ and places it on what they have added to Christ—
man-made rules, formulas, pet theories and doctrines.

Various things were added to the Gospel in the first century, and various things are added now. Basically only two
means of salvation are presented: (1) salvation by grace
through faith in Christ or (2) salvation by works. The first is
God-centered, the second is man-centered.

Even those who have experienced salvation by grace
through faith in Christ tend to look for easy formulas by
which to live the Christian life. I must admit that I have gone
through that, and I suppose almost every Christian does. We
want some rule, or regulation, to follow rather than simply
allowing the indwelling Christ to be our life.

Paul mentioned in chapter 1 the "mystery which hath
been hid from ages and from generations, but now is made
manifest to his saints" (v. 26). This mystery was "Christ in
you, the hope of glory" (v. 27). Paul used the word "mystery"
again in 2:2. Paul wanted those of Colossae and Laodicea to
"know the mystery of God, namely, Christ, in whom are
hidden all the treasures of wisdom and knowledge" (vv. 2,3,
NIV).

Paul was persuaded that the only safeguard against error
is a full knowledge of Jesus Christ. Paul greatly desired that
those of Colossae and Laodicea would grow more certain in
their knowledge of God Himself. He knew that their spiritual
experience would become richer as they understood more
fully God's great secret, which is Christ Himself. Although
people seek for the treasures of wisdom and knowledge elsewhere, these are truly found only in Jesus Christ. So the
believer's need is to have a fuller knowledge and grasp of the
Person and work of the Lord Jesus Christ. Each of us needs
to be more intensely aware that Jesus Christ was God
manifest in the flesh, and that He is all we need for time and
eternity.

The Bible emphasizes the importance of knowing Christ—
not just knowing Him as one's Saviour but gaining an intimate knowledge of Him by spending time in His Word. We
need to have the same desire the Apostle Paul had: "That I
may know him, and the power of his resurrection" (Phil.
3:10).

I came to know Christ as Saviour when I was 20 years of

age, but I have been growing in my knowledge of Him for 55 years. After all of these years, my knowledge of Him is so much more intimate now than it was at the age of 20 it is almost impossible to compare, but I am still growing in this knowledge. Paul was greatly concerned that Christians develop in their knowledge and understanding of the Person and work of Christ. We saw this previously in the Book of Colossians: "That ye might walk worthy of the Lord unto all pleasing, being fruitful in every good work, and increasing in the knowledge of God" (1:10).

Paul was also concerned that false teachers not take advantage of the Colossians. He emphasized that the Lord Jesus Christ is the One "in whom are hid all the treasures of wisdom and knowledge" (2:3). Paul then explained why he emphasized that truth: "This I say, lest any man should beguile you with enticing words. For though I be absent in the flesh, yet am I with you in the spirit, joying and beholding your order, and the stedfastness of your faith in Christ" (vv. 4,5). Concerning the false teachers, Paul added: "Beware lest any man spoil you through philosophy and vain deceit, after the tradition of men, after the rudiments of the world, and not after Christ" (v. 8).

The danger of enticing words is that they draw away from Christ, and anything that draws attention away from Christ is denounced in the Scriptures.

Another version renders verse 8: "See to it that no one takes you captive through hollow and deceptive philosophy, which depends on human tradition and the basic principles of this world rather than on Christ" (NIV).

In a sense, it is not possible to stand still in the Christian life. Either we are going forward or we are losing ground. God calls us to go forward. Hebrews 6:1 says, "Therefore leaving the principles of the doctrine of Christ, let us go on unto perfection [maturity]; not laying again the foundation of repentance from dead works, and of faith toward God." We are to rejoice in the fact that we trusted Christ as Saviour, but we are not to keep living at that level. We are to advance in the Christian life and apply the truths of God's Word to all daily situations.

Satan is deceptive, and he will do all he can to lead believers astray. What Jesus thinks of the Devil is seen from what

He said to unbelieving Jews: "Ye are of your father the devil, and the lusts of your father ye will do. He was a murderer from the beginning, and abode not in the truth, because there is no truth in him. When he speaketh a lie, he speaketh of his own: for he is a liar, and the father of it" (John 8:44).

This strong denunciation of Satan can also apply to false teachers, for they are simply the servants of Satan. But it is important that believers be able to discern which teachers are false because they come with "enticing words" (Col. 2:4). Paul also warned: "Let no man beguile you of your reward in a voluntary humility and worshipping of angels, intruding into those things which he hath not seen, vainly puffed up by his fleshly mind" (v. 18).

The Colossians had been affected by the teaching that God, who is immaterial and therefore pure, could not create a world which is material and therefore impure. The teaching was that a series of angelic beings emanated from God until at last one was far enough away from God that he could create the material universe. This led to a worship of angels. This was a particular heresy the Colossians faced, but it was no more serious than the heresies of our day that attempt to add something to the finished work of Christ. Let us never forget, Christ is all sufficient. He is all we need for salvation and victorious Christian living.

Paul also warned the believers in Rome about false teachers: "Now I beseech you, brethren, mark them which cause divisions and offences contrary to the doctrine which ye have learned; and avoid them. For they that are such serve not our Lord Jesus Christ, but their own belly; and by good words and fair speeches deceive the hearts of the simple" (Rom. 16:17,18).

Paul also warned the believers in Corinth about false teachers: "For such are false apostles, deceitful workers, tranforming themselves into the apostles of Christ. And no marvel; for Satan himself is transformed into an angel of light. Therefore it is no great thing if his ministers also be transformed as the ministers of righteousness; whose end shall be according to their works" (II Cor. 11:13-15).

Every believer needs to heed Paul's words in Ephesians 5:6: "Let no man deceive you with vain words: for because of these things cometh the wrath of God upon the children of disobedience." God has not left His own people without a means of knowing the truth. God has clearly revealed Himself in the written Word, the Bible. Each believer should be in the process of becoming more competent in knowing what the Bible says about the Person and work of God. In addition, God has also given gifted men to the Church to explain His Word and to equip believers in their tasks. Ephesians 4:11-13 says, "And he gave some, apostles; and some, prophets; and some, evangelists; and some, pastors and teachers; for the perfecting [equipping] of the saints, for the work of the ministry, for the edifying of the body of Christ: till we all come in the unity of the faith, and of the knowledge of the Son of God, unto a perfect man, unto the measure of the stature of the fulness of Christ."

The purpose of God's giving gifted men to teach His Word and equip the saints is seen from verse 14: "That we henceforth be no more children, tossed to and fro, and carried about with every wind of doctrine, by the sleight of men, and cunning craftiness, whereby they lie in wait to deceive."

The enticing words of man's philosophy and vain deceit, which Paul spoke of to the Colossians, took on several different forms. One of these forms was simply rules and regulations of men. Another was legalism—insisting on some form of ceremony under the Law system. Yet another, as we have mentioned, was the worshiping of angels because of an assumption that it was necessary to approach God through angelic beings. Some today are guilty of almost the same type of error by stating it is necessary to approach Christ through the virgin Mary. But notice what the Scriptures say: "There is one God, and one mediator between God and men, the man Christ Jesus" (I Tim. 2:5). Jesus Christ died on the cross and paid the full penalty for our sins. He is the only Mediator we need. Everyone has to approach Him in the same way—by faith in His shed blood for the forgiveness of sins.

Paul told the Colossians, "Beware lest any man spoil you" (Col. 2:8). The word translated "spoil" has the meaning of "take captive." Paul was concerned that the false teachers not carry off the Colossian believers as captives. It is a characteristic of false teachers that they do not primarily evangelize; that is, lead others to salvation in Jesus Christ.

Instead, they more commonly steal, or kidnap, those who are already young converts in established church groups. This is why it is so important for each church to ground its people in the Word of God. If the people are not grounded, it is far easier for false teachers to entice them through persuasive speech and lead them captive.

This is why over the years Back to the Bible has constantly emphasized the importance of studying the Word. The only way to recognize what is false is by knowing well what is genuine. The Bible is God's only record telling us who Jesus Christ is and what He has done for us. If the teaching of others—no matter how persuasive and how enticing—does not line up with what the Scriptures teach, then it is to be rejected.

Paul told the Colossians not to allow themselves to be taken captive "through philosophy and vain deceit, after the tradition of men" (v. 8). Another version says, "Through hollow and deceptive philosophy, which depends on human tradition" (NIV). "Tradition" refers to the handing down of customs and traditions from one generation to another, especially by word of mouth. One must always be concerned about where teaching originates. Has it originated with God or with men? A key characteristic of the cults of our day is that their teachings have originated with men, not with God.

Paul also warned the Colossians not to be taken captive "after the rudiments of the world" (v. 8). "Rudiments" refers to elementary, or basic, principles. Paul was most likely warning the Colossians about the ceremonialism associated with such things as meats, drinks and washings (see vv. 16,17). These were things that belonged to the sphere of the material and external but were not "after" or "according to" Christ (v. 8). Because Christ is all and in all, everything centers in Him. These teachers were not propagating information that lined up with truth concerning Jesus Christ and who He is; therefore, Paul warned the Colossians to have nothing to do with such teaching.

Many today wish to talk about Jesus Christ, but they avoid many of His specific teachings. But one cannot separate the Person of Christ from what He taught. If we really believe in the Person of Christ, we will believe what He taught when He said, "Except ye repent, ye shall all likewise perish" (Luke 13:3). Some think that just being kind to one's neighbor is enough, but Jesus clearly taught: "Except a man be born again, he cannot see the kingdom of God" (John 3:3). So if one is committed to the Person of Christ, he must also be committed to the teachings of Christ.

Paul also warned the Colossians: "Let no man beguile you of your reward in a voluntary humility and worshipping of angels, intruding into those things which he hath not seen, vainly puffed up by his fleshly mind" (Col. 2:18). Notice that the false teachers of Paul's day did not forsake Christ; instead, they included Him into their system of belief. Although Jesus Christ was not everything to them, the false teachers made much reference to Christ as a part of their man-made religion, and this is what was so confusing to the Colossians. The false teachers had not excluded Christ from their system of belief, but they had removed Him from His rightful place of supremacy. The false teachers were not proclaiming that Christ is all we need for salvation and the Christian life or that we may come boldly into His presence for any need we have (see Heb. 10:19-22).

In the midst of Paul's warnings to the believers in Colossae, two verses especially stand out: "As ye have therefore received Christ Jesus the Lord, so walk ye in him: rooted and built up in him, and stablished in the faith, as ye have been taught, abounding therein with thanksgiving" (Col. 2:6,7).

Paul spoke here of the necessity of the Colossians to continue as they had begun. In other words, he was telling them, "Get settled in Christ; see that Christ is everything in your life." Paul wanted the Colossians to recognize that if someone taught differently, then that teaching was in error.

We are to walk in Christ the same way as we originally received Him as our Saviour. We received Him by faith; so we are to walk in Him by faith. The way of salvation is made crystal clear in Ephesians 2:8: "For by grace are ye saved through faith; and that not of yourselves: it is the gift of God." Hebrews 11:6 says, "Without faith it is impossible to please him."

Notice that Paul used the full title for the Lord: "Christ Jesus the Lord" (Col. 2:6). "Christ" means "anointed one" or "Messiah." That is Jesus' heavenly name. "Jesus" means "one who saves" and refers to the historical Person who became flesh and lived among mankind. "Lord" means "master" and refers to His supreme control of everything.

With this threefold emphasis, Paul was reminding the Colossians whom they had become rightly related to when they received salvation. He is the Anointed One of God; He is the Saviour of mankind; He is the Supreme Lord. Paul urged the Colossians to remember that they had started with Christ by faith and that now they must continue to walk with Him by faith.

Four significant words in verse 7 become especially rich in meaning when one realizes their significance from the original language. These words are "rooted," "built," "stablished," "abounding." All four of these words in the Greek language are called "participles" because they emphasize the subject's participating in the action.

The tense of the word "rooted" emphasizes an action which has been completed and which has a continuing effect. The tense is called "perfect" because it emphasizes a perfected, or completed, act. The believers in Colossae had been rooted in Christ because they had trusted Him as their personal Saviour. Like a tree with its roots deep in the earth, the Colossians had placed their trust in Jesus Christ. Once they had done that and had become rooted in Him, there was never a need to be so rooted again.

The other three words are a different tense in the Greek language. It is known as the "present" tense, and it emphasizes action that is continuous. Therefore, the word "built" or "built up" can be translated "being built up." This word pictures the process that should be going on in each believer's life.

"Stablished" or "confirmed" also stresses continuous action—"being confirmed" in the faith. Just as building up was to be a continual process, so confirming was to be a continual process. It is not something that just takes place once and can be forgotten after that. The Christian's life should be characterized by a process of being more and more confirmed in the faith as time goes by.

"Abounding" is also a present participle, emphasizing a continual process. Since the Colossians had been rooted in Christ as Saviour, Paul wanted them to be constantly built up in Christ, confirmed in the faith and abounding in thanksgiving.

Notice the phrase in the middle of this verse: "As ye have been taught." Although Paul had not personally been to Colossae and Laodicea (see v. 1), he was well aware of the good teaching they had received and wanted them to continue in the way they had been taught. Much of Paul's information about the Colossians no doubt came from Epaphras (see 1:7,8).

Spiritual growth is impossible apart from being taught in the Word of God. This is why Paul said to the Colossians, "Let the word of Christ dwell in you richly" (3:16). It is wonderful when we have qualified instructors, but the believer is to study the Word of God for himself. A baby needs to be fed, but he should develop to the point where he is able to feed himself. So it is spiritually. When we were babes in Christ, we needed someone to feed us spiritually. However, over a period of time we should develop to the point where we can feed ourselves in the Word, while remaining open to the teaching of others. When this is the case, we will be "abounding therein with thanksgiving" (2:7). Thanksgiving is a sign of faith, and a thankful spirit is a mark of Christian maturity.

Complete Fullness

After the warnings of this portion delivered by Paul to the Colossians, we now arrive at the heart of the teaching of this book. The portion I refer to is Colossians 2:9,10: "For in him dwelleth all the fulness of the Godhead bodily. And ye are complete in him, which is the head of all principality and power."

I urge you to note the details of this passage with great care, because I am convinced the truths of this portion of God's Word can bring a dramatic change in a believer's life once they are applied. *The Scofield Reference Bible* entitles this section "Nothing can be added to completeness" (p. 1264). So we can legitimately ask, "Why, then, would we need anything else?"

Before examining these two verses in detail, let us note how some other versions translate them. "For in Him all the fulness of Deity dwells in bodily form, and in Him you have been made complete, and He is the head over all rule and authority" (NASB). Another states, "For in Christ all the fullness of the Deity lives in bodily form, and you have been given fullness in Christ, who is the head over every power and authority" (NIV). Yet another states, "For in Him the whole fullness of Deity (the Godhead), continues to dwell in bodily form—giving complete expression of the divine nature. And you are in Him, made full and have come to fullness of life—in Christ you too are filled with the Godhead: Father, Son and Holy Spirit, and reach full spiritual stature. And He is the Head of all rule and authority—of every angelic principality and power" (Amplified).

Now let us consider especially verse 9 and the first phrase of verse 10. Note that there are two distinct declarations made in these statements—the divine side and the human side. The fullness of God is in Christ. This means that everything that God is, one will also find in Christ. Christ is God, and nothing less. What God is, Christ is.

The second declaration reveals that the fullness of Christ is in the believer. This is difficult to comprehend, but it is a very special truth.

In his prayer of Colossians 1, Paul said, "[I] do not cease to pray for you, and to desire that ye might be filled with the knowledge of his will in all wisdom and spiritual understanding" (v. 9). Paul later reminded them, "Ye are complete [made full] in him" (2:10).

The central teaching of the Book of Colossians is that all the fullness of the Godhead dwells in Christ and that Christ fills the believer. Because we are identified, or united, with Him, we are one with Him. He is the Head, we are the Body.

As mentioned, Colossians 2:9,10 reveals truths that have a divine side and a human side. The "Godhead," of course, is a reference to deity, whereas the word "bodily" refers to the humanity of the Lord Jesus Christ. He took upon Himself a body at the Incarnation, and He lives in a glorified body today.

The "fulness" in verse 9 refers to the sum total of divine powers and attributes that are in Christ because He is deity. We cannot really see the true, inner essence of deity; we see only the manifestation of that essence. Romans 1:20 says, "For the invisible things of him from the creation of the world are clearly seen, being understood by the things that are made, even his eternal power and Godhead; so that they are without excuse." This verse emphasizes that created things display the attributes of the Godhead, but of course the true essence of deity is not seen. The full deity of God has been revealed to us in only one Person—the Lord Jesus Christ.

John 1:14 says, "The Word was made flesh, and dwelt among us, (and we beheld his glory, the glory as of the only begotten of the Father,) full of grace and truth." Verse 16 says, "And of his fulness have all we received, and grace for grace." Verse 18 adds, "No man hath seen God at any time; the only begotten Son, which is in the bosom of the Father, he hath declared him." Jesus Christ has given us a full revelation of God.

Referring to the Lord Jesus Christ, Hebrews 1:3 says, "Who being the brightness of his glory, and the express image of his person, and upholding all things by the word of his power, when he had by himself purged our sins, sat down on the right hand of the Majesty on high." This is the great God we have!

Matthew 1:23 reveals that Jesus Christ is God: "Behold, a virgin shall be with child, and shall bring forth a son, and they shall call his name Emmanuel, which being interpreted is, God with us." Some are willing to speak of Him as a divine being but not as God. But let it be stressed: Jesus Christ is God. He is deity. This is why Colossians 2:9 says, "In him dwelleth all the fulness of the Godhead bodily."

Colossians 1:19 says, "It pleased the Father that in him should all fulness dwell." Referring to Christ, Colossians 2:3 says, "In whom are hid all the treasures of wisdom and knowledge." Colossians 2:9 crowns these truths by revealing that the fullness of the Godhead dwells in Christ bodily.

The word translated "dwelleth" in Colossians 2:9 emphasizes being at home. It was commonly used in Bible times to refer to the permanent residence of a person. The divine fullness was not something that was added to Jesus Christ when He became a human being. Rather, it was part of His essential being from all eternity, for it permanently resides in Him. Philippians 2:6 reveals that Christ had equality with the Father before the Incarnation: "Who, being in very nature God, did not consider equality with God something to be grasped" (NIV).

The disciples realized that Jesus Christ revealed to them eternal life. The Apostle John wrote: "That which was from the beginning, which we have heard, which we have seen with our eyes, which we have looked upon, and our hands have handled, of the Word of life; (for the life was manifested, and we have seen it, and bear witness, and shew unto you that eternal life, which was with the Father, and was manifested unto us;) that which we have seen and heard declare we unto you, that ye also may have fellowship with us: and truly our fellowship is with the Father, and with his Son Jesus Christ" (I John 1:1-3).

So the fullness of the Godhead dwelt in Christ, not only before His Incarnation but also during His Incarnation. In addition, the fullness of the Godhead dwells in Him now in His glorified state in heaven. Well over 30 years had lapsed since Jesus' resurrection and ascension to the Father when Paul wrote: "In him dwelleth all the fulness of the Godhead bodily" (Col. 2:9).

"Bodily" refers to His human body, which He took upon Himself when entering the world. Hebrews 10:5 says, "Wherefore when he cometh into the world, he saith, Sacrifice and offering thou wouldest not, but a body hast thou prepared me." Philippians 2:7 refers to the same truth: "But made himself of no reputation, and took upon him the form of a servant, and was made in the likeness of men." This was the time when "the Word was made flesh, and dwelt among us" (John 1:14).

Colossians 2:3 refers to Christ "in whom are hid all the treasures of wisdom and knowledge." This shows that the fullness is hidden in Him; it is not something that is seen outwardly. This is why the religious leaders of His day missed this truth altogether. To them, Jesus was just the son of Joseph and Mary because they only perceived the physical. First Corinthians 2:14 says, "But the natural man receiveth not the things of the Spirit of God: for they are foolishness unto him: neither can he know them, because they are spiritually discerned." The religious leaders of Christ's day could not understand spiritual truths because they had never exercised faith in Christ.

Realizing that all of the fullness of the Godhead dwells in bodily form in the Lord Jesus Christ, it is then awesome to consider that we "are complete in him" (Col. 2:10). We are filled with His fullness. Notice it does not say we *ought* to be complete in Him; it says we *are* complete in Him. Of course, believers are to constantly grow in the knowledge of Him as they progress from babes in Christ to those who are spiritually mature. But the completeness exists from the moment of salvation. This is why it can be said in II Peter 1:3 that Christ "hath given unto us all things that pertain unto life and godliness."

The Apostle Paul was not content with just knowing he was complete in Christ, however. His desire was to know Christ more intimately. This desire is expressed in Philippians 3:10: "That I may know him, and the power of his resurrection." Paul knew he had not attained all that was possible for him in his day. This is why he said, "I press toward the mark for the prize of the high calling of God in Christ Jesus" (v. 14).

I have emphasized the statement "complete in Him" (Col. 2:10) because I believe it is at the very heart of Paul's letter to the Colossians. They were being confused by the false teachers of their day, but Paul wanted them to clearly understand that nothing should be added to the Person and work of the Lord Jesus Christ.

Even in our day, it is common for people to tell believers, "It is wonderful that you know Christ as Saviour and that you are endeavoring to live the Christian life the best you can, but you need something special in order to really have all that God wants you to have." They may not say it in quite these words, but this sort of teaching is causing mass confusion among Christians today. But what we need to understand is that, having trusted Jesus Christ as Saviour, we are complete in Him and need nothing else. There is no special ordinance or any special experience that needs to be tacked on to the Person and work of Christ. What can be added which the believer does not already possess in Jesus Christ? Our need is simply to appropriate what we have in Christ and thus, by faith, live accordingly.

The question might well be asked, "How, then, is this filling, or completeness, to become real in our experience?" I

believe Colossians 2:6,7 is the key to this: "As ye have therefore received Christ Jesus the Lord, so walk ye in him: rooted
and built up in him, and stablished in the faith, as ye have
been taught, abounding therein with thanksgiving." The
answer is to trust (have faith in) Jesus Christ for what is
needed in daily living. I am not referring to material sub-
stances but to power for victory over sin and power to do
what you know you should do. The first step is to know the
fullness of Christ Himself. That the believer is complete in
Christ is an eternal fact, not to be doubted nor argued. God
Himself has said it, and that should settle it for us.

Although the fullness of God is communicated to the
believer, this does not mean that the believer possesses some
of His deity. He alone possesses that. Isaiah 42:8 says, "I am
the Lord: that is my name: and my glory will I not give to
another." The believer does not possess deity, but because of
the indwelling Christ, the believer does manifest the qualities of righteousness, holiness and goodness. This is what is
meant when believers are told: "Of him are ye in Christ
Jesus, who of God is made unto us wisdom, and righteousness, and sanctification, and redemption" (I Cor. 1:30).

The righteousness which a believer possesses because of
the indwelling Christ is specifically mentioned in Romans
3:21,22: "But now the righteousness of God without the law
is manifested, being witnessed by the law and the prophets;
even the righteousness of God which is by faith of Jesus
Christ unto all and upon all them that believe." Notice that
this righteousness is given to everyone who will dare to trust,
or believe, God for salvation.

This righteousness is Christ Himself, not the changed
character of the believer nor even an attribute of God. When
a person trusts Jesus Christ as Saviour, the righteousness of
God is imputed to his account. This is what is referred to in
II Corinthians 5:21: "For he hath made him to be sin for us,
who knew no sin; that we might be made the righteousness
of God in him." Every spiritual want and every spiritual
need is fulfilled as we are in Christ. Just as one person might
deposit money as a gift to another person's bank account, so
God places the righteousness of Christ on our account when
we trust Him as our personal Saviour.

One Greek commentator says that the construction found

in verse 10 "has a strongest present connotation: 'you have been made full, are so, and continue so' " (Lenski, p. 101). Since the believer has been made full in Him, nothing further is needed. When a person appropriates all that he has in Christ and lives accordingly, he experiences the abundant Christian life.

But false teachers were troubling the Colossians and were saying that in addition to trusting Christ as Saviour they needed to observe many other regulations. Paul told the Colossians: "Let no man therefore judge you in meat, or in drink, or in respect of an holyday, or of the new moon, or of the sabbath days: which are a shadow of things to come; but the body is of Christ" (Col. 2:16,17). Paul thought the false teachers might beguile the Colossian believers of the reward that was due them (v. 18).

Complete Victory

We come to the point in the Book of Colossians which reveals that the believer's new position in Christ provides the life and power for his complete victory. This is possible in his spiritual life without adding anything to his position in Christ. No props are necessary.

Because there are those who are always wanting you to add something to your faith in order that you might be a "real" Christian, I remind you of what I suggested before. To any such people, questions should be asked such as, "Where does your teaching put Christ? Does it rob Him of the fullness of His deity? Or does it rob Him of His humanity? Does your teaching claim that the believer must have some added sentimental experience with Christ?"

Those who teach that there is some special "secret" of the Christian life present an unscriptural view and make Colossians 2:9,10 a lie. Nothing can be added to the completeness which we have in Christ. After God's creative work, He "saw every thing that he had made, and, behold, it was very good" (Gen. 1:31). God can say the same of what He has provided in Christ for the salvation and growth of every believer.

Although Jesus Christ alone is sufficient for all we need, some either do not take God at His word or they do not share with others what they know, for then they could not so easily manipulate people. For instance, many years ago I received opposition from a pastor concerning what I had said about security in Jesus Christ. He came to see me, and we discussed the matter of salvation—that it was totally of grace and that works had nothing to do with it. After our discussion, he saw my viewpoint and seemed to fully agree that the Scriptures taught what I was presenting. But then he made a statement that I have never forgotten: "But I'm not going to teach it, because I have to have an ax over my people to keep them in line." This brother refused to teach what he had agreed was the truth because he could not so easily manipulate his people. How the heart of God must be grieved with such an attitude! We do not need anything else but Jesus Christ and Him crucified, risen and living with the Father, as well as in us, today.

Colossians 2:10-15 is an elaboration of the teaching set forth in verse 9 and the first part of verse 10. This elaboration shows some practical details of what it means to be complete in Christ. We must recognize (believe) that our union with Christ gives us a new position of completeness to which nothing can be added. "Christ is all, and in all" (3:11). Therefore, it is not only unnecessary but actually sinful for anyone to get involved again with various forms of legalism, as we will see from Paul's warnings in 2:20,21.

To stress his insistence that nothing can be added to the finished work of Christ, Paul told the Colossians: "Wherefore if ye be dead with Christ from the rudiments of the world, why, as though living in the world, are ye subject to ordinances, (touch not; taste not; handle not; which all are to perish with the using;) after the commandments and doctrines of men? Which things have indeed a shew of wisdom in will worship, and humility, and neglecting of the body; not in any honour to the satisfying of the flesh" (vv. 20-23).

Separated in Christ

Having considered Paul's comments about our having been made complete in Christ, let us now consider how Paul clarified the believer's spiritual position in Christ by using several illustrations of Christ's finished work in the believer's behalf. By so doing, Paul revealed how each of us who know Christ as Saviour is complete in Him. Paul first began with an example that the believer has true circumcision in

Christ. Paul said, "In whom also ye are circumcised with the circumcision made without hands, in putting off the body of the sins of the flesh by the circumcision of Christ" (Col. 2:11).

"But," perhaps you say, "circumcision is not a rite of the Church Age; it was a rite for Old Testament Israel." That is true; however, Colossians 2:11 is not referring to a physical circumcision but a spiritual one, for it is a "circumcision made without hands." The believer's new position is that of spiritual circumcision by which he has put off the body of sin. Romans 6:6 says, "For we know that our old self was crucified with him so that the body of sin might be rendered powerless, that we should no longer be slaves to sin" (NIV). Spiritual circumcision, then, is putting off the body of sin.

In the Old Testament, circumcision was a sign of God's covenant with His chosen people, Israel. The rite was first given to Abraham, as recorded in Genesis 17:9-14. It was to be a physical operation that was to be a sign of separation. As time progressed, however, the Israelites placed more emphasis on the physical operation than they did on the spiritual significance. Thus, they ignored spiritual separation. In a sense, they were separated in the wrong way. They separated themselves from others to the extent that they did not want others to receive the Gospel. They almost stoned the Apostle Paul one time because he said he was going to the Gentiles. The Israelites had separated themselves, but they were not separated to God. God wanted them to be a spiritual light in the world to other nations, but they refused.

The Apostle Paul rebuked those who were Jews physically but not spiritually. Paul said, "For he is not a Jew, which is one outwardly; neither is that circumcision, which is outward in the flesh: but he is a Jew, which is one inwardly; and circumcision is that of the heart, in the spirit, and not in the letter; whose praise is not of man, but of God" (Rom. 2:28,29).

In the Old Testament, the spiritual significance of circumcision was emphasized as well. On one occasion, Moses told the Israelites, "Circumcise therefore the foreskin of your heart, and be no more stiffnecked" (Deut. 10:16). Also Moses said, "The Lord thy God will circumcise thine heart, and the heart of thy seed, to love the Lord thy God with all thine heart, and with all thy soul, that thou mayest live" (30:6).

Also Jeremiah 6:10 shows the spiritual significance of

circumcision: "To whom shall I speak, and give warning, that they may hear? behold, their ear is uncircumcised, and they cannot hearken: behold, the word of the Lord is unto them a reproach; they have no delight in it." And Exodus 6:12 speaks of "uncircumcised lips."

The spiritual significance of circumcision, therefore, was man's purity and his separation to God. In fact, although the circumcision rite does not carry over to Church Age believers, the word "sanctification" emphasizes the same spiritual truth. Believers are to be pure in life and separated to God—not just separated from the world but separated to God. Sanctification always carries this twofold action; that is, "from" and "unto."

This is done by trusting Christ and then recognizing that the old self has been put to death as Romans 6:6 says, "For we know that our old self was crucified with him so that the body of sin might be rendered powerless" (NIV). When Jesus Christ died, we positionally died with Him to the old nature. Although the old nature is still there because it has not been eradicated, its power over us has been broken so it cannot dominate us. The old nature will appeal to us to do and say all the wrong things. But the message of Romans 6 is that we do not have to let sin dominate us any longer. Its power over us has been broken because we have died with Christ. We are no longer slaves to the sin nature.

The truth of Romans 6:6 is applied in verses 11-13. Verses 11 and 12 say, "Likewise reckon ye also yourselves to be dead indeed unto sin, but alive unto God through Jesus Christ our Lord. Let not sin therefore reign in your mortal body, that ye should obey it in the lusts thereof." The words "let not" (v. 12), simply mean we are to say no to sin. When we say no to sin, the Holy Spirit takes over and gives us the power we need to resist. This is a benefit of the new life which we have because we are complete in Christ. To be complete in Christ, then, means He has provided everything we need to live a victorious life.

Identified With Christ

In Colossians 2, Paul first used the example of circumcision to illustrate what our completeness in Christ is like. Next, he used the example of baptism: "Buried with him in baptism, wherein also ye are risen with him through the faith of the operation of God, who hath raised him from the dead" (v. 12).

To understand better Paul's reference to baptism and resurrection, notice his statements in Romans 6:3-5: "Don't you know that all of us who were baptized into Christ Jesus were baptized into his death? We were therefore buried with him through baptism into death in order that, just as Christ was raised from the dead through the glory of the Father, we too may live a new life. If we have been united with him in his death, we will certainly also be united with him in his resurrection" (NIV).

In this portion of Scripture, the original language is very expressive in emphasizing our complete identification with Christ in His death, burial and resurrection. As one commentator states it, "We are co-buried, co-raised, and made co-alive."

In the New Testament, the word "baptize" has both a literal meaning and a figurative one. Literally, it means to "dip" or "immerse." Figuratively, it means to be "identified with." This figurative meaning is clearly seen from I Corinthians 10:2 where Paul said of the Old Testament Israelites, "[They] were all baptized unto Moses in the cloud and in the sea." As the Israelites crossed the Red Sea with Moses, they did not get a drop of water on them because they were walking across on dry ground. But they were identified with Moses as their only hope of leading them out of Egypt's slavery. From this point on, everything the Israelites were to receive from God was to come to them through Moses; so they had to be identified with him to benefit from the blessings.

This same principle is true of water baptism. No amount of water can bury a person in Christ or make him alive in Christ. However, water baptism is a picture of the believer's death, burial and resurrection with Christ. It also reveals the work of the Holy Spirit, who places us into the Body of Christ and identifies us with Christ as the Head of the Body. We receive the blessings of God because of our identification with Jesus Christ. When He was buried, positionally we were buried with Him. When He rose again, positionally we rose with Him to newness of life. All of this is brought about "through your faith in the power of God" (Col. 2:12, NIV).

The believer's identification with Christ in His death broke the power of indwelling sin; identification with Christ in His resurrection resulted in impartation of His divine nature, or life. This is what is meant when we say that we are crucified with Christ. The sin nature no longer has the power to hold us as slaves. We are to say no to sin and let the indwelling Holy Spirit energize us to do what is right.

Having died with Christ, we are endowed with His resurrection life. This is what enables the believer to live in victory over sin because He who knew no sin is in the believer to live out His resurrected life. Thus, Paul said, "And you, being dead in your sins and the uncircumcision of your flesh, hath he quickened [made alive] together with him, having forgiven you all trespasses" (v. 13).

What more do we need then? Having died to sin, having been buried and raised with Him to new life, we have complete forgiveness and a perfect standing with Him. Plus, we have Christ's life as our life for victorious living.

Two verses that especially summarize these great spiritual truths are Romans 6:4 and Galatians 2:20. Romans 6:4 says, "Therefore we are buried with him by baptism into death: that like as Christ was raised up from the dead by the glory of the Father, even so we also should walk in newness of life." Galatians 2:20 says, "I am crucified with Christ: nevertheless I live; yet not I, but Christ liveth in me: and the life which I now live in the flesh I live by the faith of the Son of God, who loved me, and gave himself for me."

Perhaps you have memorized these verses previously, but I encourage you to think of them carefully now, one phrase at a time, in order to see their full significance. And I believe you will say as I have been saying, "Christ is all we need."

Dead to the Law

As Paul continued his letter to the Colossians, he emphasized our completeness in Christ not only by referring to circumcision and baptism but also to the "handwriting of ordinances." Paul said, "Blotting out the handwriting of ordinances that was against us, which was contrary to us, and took it out of the way, nailing it to his cross" (Col. 2:14).

Another version translates this verse: "Having canceled the written code, with its regulations, that was against us and that stood opposed to us; he took it away, nailing it to the cross" (NIV).

Notice five specific statements that Paul made concerning the handwriting of ordinances: (1) He blotted it out; (2) it was against us; (3) it was contrary to us; (4) He took it out of the way; and (5) He nailed it to His cross.

Let us now consider each one of these elements. First, "blotting out the handwriting of ordinances." As previously indicated, the *New International Version* says, "Having canceled the written code, with its regulations." When the Lord Jesus Christ shed His blood for sinners, He canceled the huge debt that was against the sinner because of man's disobedience to the holy Law of God. You see, "the wages of sin is death" (Rom. 6:23). Our sin had placed us under the death penalty—not just of physical death but of spiritual death. All of us owed such a great debt it was impossible for us to pay it. But when Jesus Christ died on the cross, He canceled the debt that was against us. The written Law only revealed how far short we had come of the glory of God, but Christ canceled this because of our faith in Him.

But more than this, the Lord Jesus Christ took the Law that condemned us and set it aside so that we are no longer under its dominion. Romans 6:14 says, "For sin shall not have dominion over you: for ye are not under the law, but under grace." This does not mean that we are lawless. The believer's relationship to Law can be seen from Paul's words of I Corinthians 9:20,21: "Unto the Jews I became as a Jew, that I might gain the Jews; to them that are under the law, as under the law, that I might gain them that are under the law; to them that are without law, as without law, (being not without law to God, but under the law to Christ,) that I might gain them that are without law." Even though Paul recognized that he was no longer under the Mosaic Law of the Old Testament, he was under the law of God.

The righteousness of the Law which we could not fulfill is being fulfilled in us as we walk in the power of the Holy Spirit. Romans 8:3 says, "For what the law could not do, in that it was weak through the flesh, God sending his own Son in the likeness of sinful flesh, and for sin, condemned sin in the flesh." The purpose of this is seen in the following verse: "That the righteousness of the law might be fulfilled in us, who walk not after the flesh, but after the Spirit" (v. 4). Christ now indwells us to fulfill the Law in us.

Each believer choosing to experience spiritual victory should heed the words of Galatians 5:16-18: "So I say, live by the Spirit, and you will not gratify the desires of the sinful nature. For the sinful nature desires what is contrary to the Spirit, and the Spirit what is contrary to the sinful nature. They are in conflict with each other, so that you do not do what you want. But if you are led by the Spirit, you are not under law" (NIV).

Since each believer is complete in Christ Jesus, he is enabled to obey the Law out of love, not out of slavish fear as had been true previously. The Law still reveals God's high standard, which has never changed. We must not forget that there was nothing wrong with the Law itself but only with man's ability to meet its high demands. Christ said, "Think not that I am come to destroy the law, or the prophets: I am not come to destroy, but to fulfil" (Matt. 5:17).

But now we are identified with Christ; therefore, we are identified with what He accomplished in fulfilling the Law. This includes our standing in His righteousness and His indwelling life and power, which can enable us to live righteously in our daily experience. This is why Paul said, "I am crucified with Christ: nevertheless I live; yet not I, but Christ liveth in me" (Gal. 2:20). Because God has saved the believer, Paul also instructed: "Work out your own salvation with fear and trembling. For it is God which worketh in you both to will and to do of his good pleasure" (Phil. 2:12,13). We are to work out in daily living what God has already worked within us. No wonder Paul told believers, "Be strong in the Lord, and in the power of his might" (Eph. 6:10).

What else did Paul say about the "handwriting of ordinances" (Col. 2:14)? Not only did he say that this handwriting was blotted out by Christ, but he also said that it "was against us." This is so because it is like a hard taskmaster, commanding us to do what is right but giving us no inclination or power to accomplish what is right. Thus, as a standard it serves only as an accuser and an avenger of those who do not measure up.

Colossians 2:14 also indicates that "the handwriting of ordinances . . . was contrary to us." Why is the Mosaic Law considered to be contrary to us? Because it is impossible for us to satisfy God's requirements in the power we humanly possess; God's standards cannot be kept in our own strength. The standards are enormously high because they are God's standards and are as holy as He is holy. When we see ourselves so far short of being able to keep such high standards, we realize those standards are "contrary to us" (v. 14).

Observe a fourth element about the handwriting of ordinances: Christ "took it out of the way" (v. 14). The question might be asked, "Did God change His mind because He saw that man could not keep His high standards?" No. God did not make His standards lower just because man could not keep them. God's righteousness had to be satisfied, and He will not lower His standards for anyone. But the good news, or the Gospel, is that although we could not meet these high standards, Christ gave Himself for us on the cross. He took the handwriting of ordinances out of the way by fulfilling the Law and fully paying the penalty of our sin. He paid our full debt.

Notice what else Christ did to the handwriting of ordinances: He took it out of the way, "nailing it to his cross" (v. 14). Based on the original language, the word "nailing" should be literally translated "having nailed." This indicates the means by which Jesus Christ paid our full debt—He nailed it to the cross.

This emphasizes that Christ fully met the demands of the Law. Jesus said He came to fulfill the Law and added, "For verily I say unto you, Till heaven and earth pass, one jot or one tittle shall in no wise pass from the law, till all be fulfilled" (Matt. 5:18). Jesus spoke these words before He went to the cross because, even then, He was fulfilling the Law by His completely righteous life. Then on the cross, He fulfilled the Law for us by taking our full penalty upon Himself. So He took the handwriting that was against us out of the way, having nailed it to the cross. The Lord Jesus Christ perfectly kept the Law while He lived among men and proved He was the perfect substitute for our sin. He was the only One who could die for the sins of others because He had no sin Himself. Having personally fulfilled the Law Himself, the Lord

Jesus Christ then liberated us from the condemnation of the Law by His death in our place. This is why Romans 8:1 says, "There is therefore now no condemnation to them which are in Christ Jesus." Since Christ not only fulfilled the demands of the Law for Himself but also for us, He won a double victory.

Because Jesus Christ has paid our full penalty, we will never be called into question again. Even as a criminal who has paid the penalty for a broken law is not punished again, so the Lord Jesus Christ has paid our full penalty, and we will never again come into condemnation. When Jesus Christ fulfilled the Law by His own righteous life and by dying for our sins, this brought an end to the Age of Law. When Christ died, "the veil of the temple was rent in twain from the top to the bottom" (Matt. 27:51). This symbolic miracle indicated that everyone now had direct access to God. It was no longer necessary to come through the Jewish nation or by means of the Old Testament Law. Everyone is now able to come boldly into the presence of God by the blood of Jesus Christ (see Heb. 10:19-22).

It should be remembered, however, that the purpose of the Law was never to provide salvation. In his letter to the Galatians, Paul had a great deal to say about the Law because some of the Galatians thought one needed to add the keeping of the Law to faith in Jesus Christ. Paul wrote: "Wherefore then serveth the law? It was added because of transgressions, till the seed should come to whom the promise was made; and it was ordained by angels in the hand of a mediator" (3:19). The phrase "it was added because of transgressions" indicates the Law was given in order to make sin more easily recognizable and more clearly defined.

For instance, suppose there were signs on our interstate highway system that indicated speed should be "reasonable and safe." Some would drive 55 miles an hour, some 65, some 75—and some faster. When a highway patrolman would stop a person driving too fast for the road conditions, there could be a sharp difference of opinion about what is "reasonable and safe." Thus, the law has been made specific so that none need wonder what the limit is. Because some would abuse the system and would lack judgment in what is "reasonable and safe," the law "was added because of transgressions."

Galatians 3:19 also emphasizes that the Law was added "till the seed should come to whom the promise was made." This set a time limit on the Law. It had a definite beginning— "it was added" implies there was a time when it did not exist. And it had a definite end—"till the seed should come."

At least 2500 years of man's history elapsed before the Law was given through Moses. Until that time, when men transgressed, there were few specific laws to condemn them. But the Law was added in order that transgression might be recognizable and specific.

But there was also a time limit! The Mosaic Law was never intended to be in effect forever. It was added "till the seed should come" (v. 19), which is a reference to the Lord Jesus Christ.

Thus, Galatians 3:24,25 says, "Wherefore the law was our schoolmaster to bring us unto Christ, that we might be justified by faith. But after that faith is come, we are no longer under a schoolmaster." In verse 24, the words "to bring us" are in italics in the King James Version, indicating they were added by the translators to give a clearer understanding of what was intended by the Greek construction in the verse. However, these words which have been added to this verse can also be misleading. The verse reads literally: "The law has become our trainer unto Christ with Christ's coming in view." This indicates the precise time limit.

Verse 25 reveals, "But after that faith is come, we are no longer under a schoolmaster." The Law system was not only in effect until the coming of Christ, but it also brings an individual to see his need of placing faith in Christ because the person becomes aware he cannot meet God's standards in his own strength. But once faith is exercised, the Law has served its purpose and the individual is "no longer under a schoolmaster." Therefore, Paul's words to the Galatians— and all believers—were: "Stand fast therefore in the liberty wherewith Christ hath made us free, and be not entangled again with the yoke of bondage" (5:1). That is, once you are free from the Law system because you have placed your faith in Christ, do not try to be justified by keeping the Law.

Paul further said, "Christ is become of no effect unto you,

whosoever of you are justified by the law; ye are fallen from grace. For we through the Spirit wait for the hope of righteousness by faith" (vv. 4,5). Thus, we see that the words "fallen from grace" apply specifically to those people who are seeking to be justified by the works of the Law rather than by faith in Jesus Christ alone. This is because all that Christ has accomplished is of no effect to the person who is endeavoring to be justified by the works of the Law. Such a person has simply put himself back under the bondage of the Law system rather than accepting what Christ has done in his behalf. Such a person has nullified the finished work of Christ on the cross.

"But," someone may say, "if I don't keep the Law or have the Law before me all the time, I'll feel as if I can sin and nothing will bother me." Paul also knew about that and exhorted, "Ye have been called unto liberty; only use not liberty for an occasion to the flesh, but by love serve one another" (v. 13). Paul also urged, "Walk in the Spirit, and ye shall not fulfil the lust of the flesh" (v. 16). Verse 18 assures, "If ye be led of the Spirit, ye are not under the law." And verse 25 reminds us, "If we live in the Spirit, let us also walk in the Spirit."

What we have been saying about the Law has direct bearing on what is said in Romans 8:3,4: "For what the law could not do, in that it was weak through the flesh, God sending his own Son in the likeness of sinful flesh, and for sin, condemned sin in the flesh: that the righteousness of the law might be fulfilled in us, who walk not after the flesh, but after the Spirit." There is nothing wrong with the Law itself, only with our ability to fulfill it. But Christ fulfilled it for us and now lives in us to work out His perfect life through us. In other words, if we walk in the Spirit, we shall fulfill the law of Christ and not fulfill the sinful things of the world. What wonderful provisions God has made for us so we can stand fast in the liberty Christ made available.

Dead to Satan

In addition to all that Colossians 2:14 says Christ accomplished for us, verse 15 says, "Having spoiled principalities and powers, he made a shew of them openly, triumphing over them in it." Here we see Christ's total victory over the powers of evil. He completely stripped the powers of Satan and the demons.

Ephesians 6:12 reveals we are involved in a spiritual warfare: "We wrestle not against flesh and blood, but against principalities, against powers, against the rulers of the darkness of this world, against spiritual wickedness in high places." When the Lord Jesus Christ died on the cross for us, He broke Satan's power over us.

Christ's victory over Satan is recorded in Hebrews 2:14: "Forasmuch then as the children are partakers of flesh and blood, he also himself likewise took part of the same; that through death he might destroy him that had the power of death, that is, the devil." This spells out the full emancipation which Christ accomplished for us.

Having dealt with our sins and the Law on the cross, Christ also dealt with Satan and his demons. During His time on earth, Jesus prophesied that He would judge the prince of this world: "Now is the judgment of this world: now shall the prince of this world be cast out" (John 12:31). Satan may have felt that he triumphed over Christ when the Saviour died on the cross, but in turn Satan discovered what a great defeat he had suffered, from which he will never be able to recover.

The statement "having spoiled principalities and powers" (Col. 2:15) reveals that Christ disarmed Satan, including all of the evil powers and authorities associated with him. The satanic armies of principalities and powers have been disgraced through defeat. Of course, it is necessary for the believer to claim the victory, by faith, in order to benefit from what Christ accomplished on the cross. This is where the believer needs to "be strong in the Lord, and in the power of his might" (Eph. 6:10).

In Joshua's time the Israelites were commanded to take the land for it to be theirs (Josh. 1:2,3). Now believers must personally appropriate the available blessings in order for those blessings to be of benefit. In a sense, God was telling Joshua, "I have given you this whole land, but you must go in and take it." So also, God is telling the believer, "I have given you all these blessings, but you must appropriate them for yourself in order for them to do you any good."

Concerning principalities and powers, Colossians 2:15

says that Christ "made a shew of them openly, triumphing
over them in it." Another translation says, "He made a
public spectacle of them, triumphing over them by the cross"
(NIV). No doubt at first Satan thought he had triumphed
when Christ was crucified and buried. But by the power of
God, Christ was resurrected, ascended to heaven, and is now
seated at the right hand of the Father. Thus, God was completely vindicated, and Satan was completely thwarted. The
Devil and his armies were completely conquered, and their
power was absolutely broken. This is why when we take our
stand in Christ and use the spiritual armor (Eph. 6:13-17),
Satan cannot harm us. God may allow him to test us—even
as He allowed him to test Job—but God will never allow
Satan to overcome us as we walk in dependence on Him. We
are complete in Him and have all we need to live in victory
over Satan and sin. So we need to heed the words of Scripture: "Walk in the Spirit, and ye shall not fulfil the lust of the
flesh" (Gal. 5:16). Also, "that the righteousness of the law
might be fulfilled in us, who walk not after the flesh, but after
the Spirit" (Rom. 8:4).

Christ triumphed over principalities and powers by means
of the cross. That is what is meant by "in it" (Col. 2:15).
Christ's victorious entrance into glory after the resurrection
indicates the extent of His triumph. As the Roman generals
of the first century returned triumphantly from the battle
and distributed gifts to the soldiers, so Christ entered heaven
triumphantly and gave gifted men to the Church. Ephesians
4:8 says, "Therefore it is said, When He ascended on high, He
led captivity captive—He led a train of vanquished foes—
and He bestowed gifts on men" (Amplified).

Because of all that Jesus Christ has accomplished for us,
we can say with the Apostle Paul, "Now thanks be unto God,
which always causeth us to triumph in Christ" (II Cor. 2:14).
Because the triumph of Christ makes it possible for us to be
victorious, Paul said, "Therefore, my beloved brethren, be ye
stedfast, unmoveable, always abounding in the work of the
Lord, forasmuch as ye know that your labour is not in vain in
the Lord" (I Cor. 15:58). How wonderful it is to realize that
because we are complete in Christ He gives us the power we
need to triumph over evil because He triumphed over evil on
the cross.

Chapter 7

Liberty in Christ Challenged

Paul wrote to the believers in Colossae about their perfect position in Christ and the liberty they had as a result. But because this liberty was challenged, Paul gave three specific warnings that can be categorized as: Let no one judge you (Col. 3:16,17); let no man beguile you (vv. 18,19); and let no man enslave you (vv. 20-23). The first two statements come directly from verses 16 and 18, and the third statement sums up the sense of what Paul expressed in his third warning.

This threefold warning indicates that Christian liberty was being challenged from three different angles. Keep in mind as we speak of liberty that we are referring to being freed from the bondage of sin to serve the Lord. Before salvation, a person is a slave to sin, but after salvation the believer is free to please the Lord. The old self is still there with its drawing power, but the believer has the strength of the indwelling Christ to overcome sin. The believer has the privilege of saying yes to Christ and no to sin—a choice which no unbeliever has because he is enslaved to sin.

"Let No Man . . . Judge You"

From Paul's warnings to the Colossians, we can surmise the kinds of attacks that were being made on their Christian liberty. Paul's first warning was "Let no man therefore judge you in meat, or in drink, or in respesct of an holyday, or of the new moon, or of the sabbath days: which are a shadow of things to come; but the body is of Christ" (Col. 2:16,17).

The word "therefore" (v. 16) relates to the preceding verses. Paul had told the Colossians—and all believers— that all the fullness of God dwelt in Jesus Christ bodily and that believers are complete in Christ. Paul then used illustrations to show that a believer has died to the dominion of sin and that the Law can no longer dominate or condemn. Paul also showed that the powers of Satan have been broken. Paul referred to all of this background information when he said, "Let no man therefore judge you" (v. 16). Since nothing can be added to the believer's perfect standing in Jesus Christ, he is not to let anyone judge, beguile or enslave him.

Paul's warning to the Colossians would be like warning the Old Testament Israelites, "Don't let the Egyptians enslave you again." How could the Egyptians enslave them? Only by the Israelites' going back to Egypt. Although the power of Egypt had been broken, the nation still existed. So Paul was telling the Colossians not to return to the sins which had previously enslaved them. Each believer still has an old nature even though its power has been broken, and Paul did not want the Colossians to allow their sin nature to dominate them again.

It is evident from Colossians 2:16 that some were judging the Colossians in the matters Paul mentioned: "In meat, or in drink, or in respect of an holyday, or of the new moon, or of the sabbath days." The believer has been fully accepted by Christ and is complete in Him; therefore, he is not to let anyone judge him in matters of food, special feast days or sabbath days. These matters do not make a person more holy or more Christian. Having trusted Christ as Saviour, the believer has all he needs for spiritual life and victory.

God's kingdom is not composed of food and drink—these are important but secondary. Romans 14:17 says, "For the kingdom of God is not meat and drink; but righteousness, and peace, and joy in the Holy Ghost [Spirit]." Concerning special foods, Paul said, "Let not him that eateth despise him that eateth not; and let not him which eateth not judge him that eateth: for God hath received him" (v. 3). Concerning special days, Paul said, "One man esteemeth one day above another: another esteemeth every day alike. Let every man be fully persuaded in his own mind. He that regardeth the day, regardeth it unto the Lord; and he that regardeth not the day, to the Lord he doth not regard it" (vv. 5,6).

Paul further stated, "So then every one of us shall give account of himself to God. Let us not therefore judge one another any more: but judge this rather, that no man put a

stumblingblock or an occasion to fall in his brother's way"
(vv. 12,13).

The Christian's Liberty

Romans 14 is a key chapter dealing with Christian liberty.
Those matters which Paul was discussing were those which
the Scriptures had not spoken specifically for or against. As
such, believers had to decide what they would do concerning
them, and Paul was giving guidelines in this chapter.
Another chapter to study in this same regard is I Corinthians 8. But I repeat, the area being considered had to do with
those things about which the Scriptures had not spoken
clearly for or against. This is the area of Christian liberty.
Paul emphasized that Christians shouldn't set themselves
up as judges over other Christians. So Paul told the Colossians, "Let no man therefore judge you in meat, or in drink,
or in respect of an holyday, or of the new moon, or of the
sabbath days" (Col. 2:16). During the time when the Old
Testament Law was in effect, these were very important
matters. But Jesus Christ completely fulfilled the Law by
His righteous life and paid the penalty for us by dying on the
cross, so these Old Testament matters are no longer significant.

Paul's reference to "an holyday, or of the new moon, or of
the sabbath days" most likely referred to special days and
times associated with the Old Testament Law. Since the
Colossian believers were no longer under the Law system, it
was not necessary for them to keep these special regulations.

Although there is little debate today about Old Testament
days and special times, one does occasionally hear debates
about the believer's attitude toward Christmas and Easter. I
believe God would tell us the same thing concerning these
days that Paul told the Colossians about special days. If one
wishes to observe them, it is not a sin. If one wishes not to
observe them, that is not a sin either. It is important, however, that each believer remember the virgin birth and also
the resurrection of the Lord Jesus Christ. Whether that is
done at a specific time or throughout the year is not important enough to fight over.

The "sabbath days" (v. 16) which Paul mentioned have
been misunderstood by many during this Church Age. The

command to keep the Sabbath has never been given to the Gentiles; in fact, it was never given to the Jews until Exodus 20. But even then, the Sabbath specifically related to God's covenant with Israel. Exodus 31:13 says, "Speak thou also unto the children of Israel, saying, Verily my sabbaths ye shall keep: for it is a sign between me and you throughout your generations; that ye may know that I am the Lord that doth sanctify you." Notice also verses 16,17: "Wherefore the children of Israel shall keep the sabbath, to observe the sabbath throughout their generations, for a perpetual covenant. It is a sign between me and the children of Israel for ever."

From these verses it is clear that the command to keep the Sabbath was given to the Jewish nation, not to the Gentiles, for God had made no such covenant with the Gentiles.

Also it is not proper to speak of Sunday as the "Christian Sabbath" because the Sabbath was given only to Israel. When the Israelites rejected Jesus Christ as their Messiah, God temporarily set aside His program with the nation. During the Church Age, there is no emphasis on a Sabbath because God is not working with Israel as such. Even in New Testament times, believers of the Church Age customarily met on the first day of the week, which we refer to as Sunday. Acts 20:7 states, "Upon the first day of the week, when the disciples came together to break bread, Paul preached unto them." Paul also encouraged the act of giving on the first day of the week: "Upon the first day of the week let every one of you lay by him in store, as God hath prospered him" (I Cor. 16:2). During New Testament times, born-again Gentiles did not meet on the seventh day of the week but on the first day of the week. No doubt the first day of the week was chosen as a meeting time because it commemorated the victorious resurrection of Jesus Christ (see John 20:1,19). Also a careful comparison of the Old Testament feast days (Lev. 23) with Acts 2 indicates the Holy Spirit came on the first day of the week to found the Church.

Even though the Church is not bound by the Sabbath Day as Israel was, there are some valid principles we can gain from God's institution of the Sabbath. For instance, Jesus said, "The sabbath was made for man, and not man for the sabbath" (Mark 2:27). The Sabbath was instituted for the benefit of man. I believe this verse teaches the principle that man needs at least one day of rest in seven in order to allow his physical, mental and emotional powers to recuperate. What more refreshing way could one do this than spending time with fellow Christians who love the Lord Jesus Christ? Spiritual refreshment comes as we study the Word of God together and share what Jesus Christ has done in each other's lives. This gives us the encouragement we need to go back out into the world to reach the lost for Christ.

Paul explained to the Colossians why the special regulations of Old Testament times were no longer binding on believers: "Which are a shadow of things to come; but the body is of Christ" (Col. 2:17). The special regulations of the Old Testament pointed to Christ, but now that He has come one no longer needs to cling to those things which only pointed to Him. We now have Jesus Christ Himself, and we are complete in Him.

The Law's Value

"What then," some may ask, "is the value of Old Testament Law now?" Even though we are not under its regulations, the Law still performs various ministries today. First, the Law still reveals the holiness of God, which we need to be reminded of. Second, the Law reveals Jesus Christ to us (see Luke 24:27,44), even though we now have a complete revelation in the New Testament.

Third, the Bible tells us, "The law is good, if a man use it lawfully" (I Tim. 1:8). To use it "lawfully" is to use it properly, or for the use it was intended.

A fourth ministry of the Law is related to the third: The Law reveals sin and warns of its consequences. The Law was never intended to provide salvation to those who keep it. This is clear from Romans 3:20: "Therefore no one will be declared righteous in his sight by observing the law; rather, through the law we become conscious of sin" (NIV). Thus, the lawful use of the Law, or using it for its intended purpose, is to use the Law to point out sin by showing the high standards of God. It is not using the Law properly if one claims that salvation comes from keeping it or that spiritual maturity comes from keeping it.

Fifth, the Law reveals man's inability to become saved by

works and casts him upon the grace of God for salvation. The Law has no power to prevent sin, nor has it any power to redeem the sinner. The means of salvation is clearly seen from Ephesians 2:8,9: "For by grace are ye saved through faith; and that not of yourselves: it is the gift of God: not of works, lest any man should boast." No wonder Paul could tell the Colossians that the special regulations of the law "are a shadow of the things that were to come; the reality, however, is found in Christ" (Col. 2:17, NIV; see also Heb. 10:1).

"Let No Man Beguile You"

Paul then gave a second warning to the believers in Colossae: "Let no man beguile you of your reward in a voluntary humility and worshipping of angels, intruding into those things which he hath not seen, vainly puffed up by his fleshly mind, and not holding the Head, from which all the body by joints and bands having nourishment ministered, and knit together, increaseth with the increase of God" (Col. 2:18,19).

Paul didn't want anyone to beguile the Colossians of their reward; that is, he did not want anyone to cheat them out of their joy or the prize which they had in Christ Jesus. They were complete in Christ, as all believers are, and Paul did not want to see their joy diminished in any way.

Let's look at other translations of the phrase, "Let no man beguile you." One says, "Let no one keep defrauding you" (NASB). Another states it similarly: "Let no one defraud you" (Amplified). Yet another says, "Do not let anyone . . . disqualify you" (NIV).

Verses 18 and 19 serve as a strong reminder of what we possess by being "in Christ." The fullness of the Godhead dwells in Christ bodily, and we are complete in Him (vv. 9,10). Some were falsely teaching, however, that man is too unworthy to approach God through Christ directly. They taught it was necessary for man to approach God through the mediation of angels. Thus, Paul's reference to "worshipping of angels" (v. 18). Paul said that these false teachers had a "voluntary humility"; that is, they were proud of their humility.

Those who seek to come to Christ through mediators—

whether angels as taught in the first century or the virgin
Mary and saints as taught in the 20th century—lay themselves open to counterfeit experiences. This is also true of
those who say we should have some special experience. This
leaves people wide open for Satan to give an imitation experience of some kind and for people to claim, "Now I've got it"
when they receive nothing from God at all. Because the
believer is complete in Christ (v. 10), he has all he needs for
righteousness and victorious living. No special experience is
needed.

Those who teach the necessity of coming to Christ through
a mediator deny the plain teaching of the Scriptures. God
has made it possible for us to come directly into His presence
by Jesus Christ. Hebrews 10:19,20 states, "Having therefore,
brethren, boldness to enter into the holiest by the blood of
Jesus, by a new and living way, which he hath consecrated
for us, through the veil, that is to say, his flesh." Hebrews
4:16 states, "Let us therefore come boldly unto the throne of
grace, that we may obtain mercy, and find grace to help in
time of need."

In spite of what was taught in the first century, angels are
not for mediation between God and man. Instead, angels
minister to believers. Hebrews 1:14 says of angels, "Are they
not all ministering spirits, sent forth to minister for them
who shall be heirs of salvation?" That no mediator—of any
kind—is needed other than Jesus Christ is clear from
I Timothy 2:5: "For there is one God, and one mediator
between God and men, the man Christ Jesus." The same
truth was emphasized by Jesus Himself, who said, "No man
cometh unto the Father, but by me" (John 14:6). Our access
to the Father is also seen from Romans 5:1,2: "Therefore
being justified by faith, we have peace with God through our
Lord Jesus Christ: by whom also we have access by faith
into this grace wherein we stand, and rejoice in hope of the
glory of God."

Even though we are encouraged to come boldly to the
throne of grace directly through Jesus Christ, this does not
mean that we are to come with a haughty, or proud, spirit.

Those who teach that Jesus Christ must be approached
through mediators are completely ignoring our true position
in Christ. They are not submitting to the authority of the

Word of God. Any person who attempts to reach God the Father through anyone other than Jesus Christ is an idolater in the scriptural sense of the word.

It is interesting to study examples in the Scriptures of how people were humbled as they came into the presence of God. Job is one such example. At first, he was proud of the way he had served God, but after the events of the book had transpired, Job was utterly humbled before God. Finally, Job said to God, "I have heard of thee by the hearing of the ear: but now mine eye seeth thee. Wherefore I abhor myself, and repent in dust and ashes" (Job 42:5,6).

Isaiah is another example. When he saw the glory of the Lord, he was so humbled and became so insignificant in his own eyes he thought he might die. Isaiah 6 records the vision and call of Isaiah. The humility which he experienced is seen particularly in verse 5: "Then said I, Woe is me! for I am undone; because I am a man of unclean lips, and I dwell in the midst of a people of unclean lips: for mine eyes have seen the King, the Lord of hosts."

The Apostle John is another example. John had been banished to the Isle of Patmos where he received a vision and revelation of Jesus Christ, which he recorded in the Book of the Revelation. The first chapter records the magnificent vision which John saw. Verse 17 reveals how humbled he was: "And when I saw him, I fell at his feet as dead. And he laid his right hand upon me, saying unto me, Fear not; I am the first and the last."

Because of the believer's complete standing in Christ, Paul did not want the Colossians to let anyone rob them of their spiritual rights. On the surface, claiming that one has to approach Jesus Christ through angelic beings might seem the humble position to take. But Paul pointed out that this was a "voluntary humility" (Col. 2:18), which in fact was contrary to the teaching of God's Word. Such an attitude would involve the believer in the error of not holding fast to the Head of his faith: "And not holding the Head, from which all the body by joints and bands having nourishment ministered, and knit together, increaseth with the increase of God" (v. 19).

The person who thinks he needs to approach God by a mediator other than Jesus Christ has lost connection with the Head of the Body. Not only does such a view hurt the individual, but it is also disloyal to Christ. Only when the absolute supremacy of Christ is adhered to can the Body (the Church) function normally and grow. The parallel is to the human body whose head must direct its functions. Only as believers receive directions from their Head will they be properly nourished, strengthened and knit together.

Let No One Enslave You

Paul emphasized the supremacy of Christ when he said, "Wherefore if ye be dead with Christ from the rudiments of the world, why, as though living in the world, are ye subject to ordinances" (Col. 2:20). Verses 20-23 emphasize that the believer is emancipated and is not to allow himself to be enslaved again.

In verse 20, Paul stated that the believers were "dead with Christ." Death always means separation, and here it refers to a separation from the rudiments of this world. Death also is final. These believers did not need to die with Christ again; they had died with Christ but were now alive to God.

The "rudiments of the world" refers to the basic principles of the world system. It is a purely material way of viewing things. The Colossians had been delivered from that viewpoint, and Paul did not want them to be enslaved again. *The Amplified Bible* translates verse 20: "If then you have died with Christ to material ways of looking at things and have escaped from the world's crude and elemental notions and teachings of externalism, why do you live as if you still belong to the world?—Why do you submit to rules and regulations?"

It is important for the believer to recognize that his death with Christ is an absolute fact, not something one hopes to obtain by some experience. For the believer, it is something that occurred in the past, for it took place when he trusted Jesus Christ as his personal Saviour. We have made frequent reference to Romans 6 in this regard, and I encourage you to read the portion again with this great truth in mind. Verses 3-5 reveal that we have experienced death, burial and resurrection with Jesus Christ. Verse 11 indicates that we are to "reckon" on these facts; that is, count them as true and live accordingly. Verses 12,13 emphasize that we should say yes to the things of righteousness and no to the things of unrighteousness. We do this by yielding, or presenting, our members to God for His will rather than using them for sinful practices. In this same regard, Romans 12:1 says, "I beseech you therefore, brethren, by the mercies of God, that ye present your bodies a living sacrifice, holy, acceptable unto God, which is your reasonable service."

A believer has been delivered from the legalism of the world system, from the prohibitions that are purely human in origin. His desire should be to glorify Jesus Christ in all that he does.

He must especially recognize that his body is a temple of the Holy Spirit because the Spirit indwells him. This truth is especially seen in I Corinthians 6:19: "What? know ye not that your body is the temple of the Holy Ghost [Spirit] which is in you, which ye have of God, and ye are not your own?" This means we need to take care of our bodies by having proper habits of eating and exercise. Some eat too much and become overweight; others drink too much coffee or cola and become nervous; others do not exercise and become lethargic. I suppose each of us does better in one of these areas than in the others, but as believers our concern should be to have proper habits in all areas.

Each believer needs to have bodily discipline. Paul said, "I keep under my body, and bring it into subjection" (9:27). He also said, "Bodily exercise profiteth little" (I Tim. 4:8); that is, it profits only a little in contrast to what righteousness profits, but bodily exercise does profit a little. We should not go to an extreme in physical exercise, but some exercise is profitable—even necessary—in properly caring for the temple of God.

Although there is a place for proper bodily care, all of this accomplishes nothing for our spiritual life. It has no sanctifying value. Just as keeping or not keeping certain days does not have sanctifying value to the Christian life, neither does adhering to a certain type of diet have sanctifying value. For instance, many people give up certain enjoyments for Lent, and although the special diets and other regulations may make them feel spiritual, they add absolutely nothing to one's spiritual life. We are complete in Christ if we have trusted Him as our personal Saviour. Now our responsibility is simply to live out His life which is in us.

Consider a comparison between our physical and spiritual lives. Even though one needs certain regulations concerning his physical being, his body does not operate by laws, rules and regulations. For instance, when sitting down to a meal, it is not necessary to tell your body to start digesting food nor to tell your heart and lungs to continue operating at a certain rate per minute. It is important that you get physical nourishment and take proper care of your body, but life is not sustained by regulations.

In the same way, the Christian life is not run by regulations. From Colossians 2:9,10 we have seen that Christ is our life and that we are complete in Him. Therefore, we should not endeavor to maintain our spiritual lives by regulations which are based on the world system. Obeying man-made religious regulations might seem outwardly spiritual, but it does not add to the spiritual life. In fact, Colossians 2:23 says, "Which things have indeed a shew of wisdom in will worship, and humility, and neglecting of the body; not in any honour to the satisfying of the flesh." Another translation says, "Such regulations indeed have an appearance of wisdom, with their self-imposed worship, their false humility and their harsh treatment of the body, but they lack any value in restraining sensual indulgence" (NIV).

Man-made regulations do not control or overcome the flesh. A believer may say to his flesh, "Don't tempt me any more," but the flesh will tempt him anyway. So it is important to understand that man-made discipline may be attractive, but it is unable to bring the flesh under control. It is actually an endeavor to control the flesh by means of the flesh. This is impossible.

The solution is given in Galatians 5:16: "This I say then, Walk in the Spirit, and ye shall not fulfil the lust of the flesh." To the person who asks, "Why is this necessary?" Paul answered, "For the flesh lusteth against the Spirit, and the Spirit against the flesh: and these are contrary the one to the other: so that ye cannot do the things that ye would. But if ye be led of the Spirit, ye are not under the law" (vv. 17,18).

Some of the Galatian believers were trying to grow in the Christian life by means of regulations and works, even though they recognized that salvation was through the Holy Spirit. Paul asked them, "Are ye so foolish? having begun in the Spirit, are ye now made perfect [mature] by the flesh?" (3:3).

Occasionally, when one recognizes his liberty in Christ, he is not as concerned as he should be about a separated life. So Paul warned, "Brethren, ye have been called unto liberty; only use not liberty for an occasion to the flesh, but by love serve one another" (5:13).

In his letter to the Colossians, Paul was specific in his questioning: "Wherefore if [since] ye be dead with Christ from the rudiments of the world, why, as though living in the world, are ye subject to ordinances?" (2:20). Paul was not counseling the Colossians to become rebels, but he was warning them not to think they were spiritual because they obeyed certain rules and regulations that pertain to the body.

Although the believer is not to participate in anything that is sinful, he needs to see other things in life as provided by God for his enjoyment. Paul told Timothy: "Charge them that are rich in this world, that they be not highminded, nor trust in uncertain riches, but in the living God, who giveth us richly all things to enjoy" (I Tim. 6:17). Many Christians give the impression by the way they live that God does not want us to enjoy anything. And that was the case in Colossae. Greek philosophy had taught that material things were evil; therefore, even some of the believers had the wrong attitude toward their physical body. They set up a system of denials concerning it, thinking that would add to their spirituality.

Paul told Timothy some of the things that would be done by false teachers in the latter days: "Forbidding to marry, and commanding to abstain from meats, which God hath created to be received with thanksgiving of them which believe and know the truth. For every creature of God is good, and nothing to be refused, if it be received with thanksgiving" (4:3,4).

Although we do not run our spiritual lives by regulations, Paul gave certain guidelines to help believers know what to do when they are uncertain (see Rom. 14; I Cor. 8). We should not use our Christian liberty in such a way that others who do not understand would be hindered in their spiritual growth. We are not to be a stumbling block to them. But when it comes to the matter of abstaining from particular foods or observing particular days, the Scriptures make it clear that those who do are not more spiritual than those who do not.

In writing to the Colossians about such ordinances, Paul described them as "Touch not; taste not; handle not" (Col. 2:21). They are of such a temporary nature that they have no importance to the spiritual life (see v. 22).

Paul further said about such ordinances, "Which things have indeed a shew of wisdom in will worship, and humility, and neglecting of the body; not in any honour to the satisfying of the flesh" (v. 23). Paul's warning in verse 18 was against mysticism ("intruding into those things which he hath not seen"), and his warning in verse 23 was against asceticism ("neglecting of the body").

Ascetic practices for religious reasons have deceptive value. Those who follow such rules and regulations feel they are more spiritual, although they are not. There is to be a denial in the Christian life, but this denial relates to self, not to the comforts of the physical body. Jesus said, "If any man will come after me, let him deny himself, and take up his cross daily, and follow me" (Luke 9:23). The person who has trusted Jesus Christ as Saviour needs to deny his old self, recognizing that he has died with Christ to the flesh. The believer is to deny those things that characterized his old life.

In Colossians, however, the issue seems to have been that of denying oneself physical comforts because they considered the body to be evil. This concept is totally out of line with the truth of God's Word. By denying themselves physical comforts, these false teachers thought one could restrain his sensual desires. Paul, however, made it clear that "such regulations indeed have an appearance of wisdom, with their self-imposed worship, their false humility and their harsh treatment of the body, but they lack any value in restraining sensual indulgence" (Col. 2:23, NIV).

Paul clearly pointed out that ascetic practices for religious purposes are really a mark of pride, and they set aside the finished work of Christ on our behalf. Such an attitude nulli-

fies what has been set forth in 2:9,10—that all the fullness of
the Godhead dwells in Christ bodily and that we are complete in Him. Our only hope for spiritual maturity is to
appropriate what we have in Him.

Paul referred to the ascetic practices as "a shew of wisdom
in will worship, and humility" (v. 23). Notice, it was only a
show of humility. However, when we accept God's grace for
salvation and forgiveness of sin, we experience true
humility, and God is exalted in our lives.

It is regrettable that the people who practice asceticism
often have a reputation for spirituality, but the true product
is missing. Such people develop a reputation, but it is only
skin deep. Here are some thoughts about reputation which I
have appreciated: "Reputation is what others suppose we
are; character is what we really are." "Reputation is seem-
ing; character is being." "Reputation is your photograph;
character is your face." "Reputation is what men think you
are; character is what God knows you are." These thoughts
are from *The Cream Sentence Sermons Book,* compiled by
Keith L. Brooks, which I have much appreciated for its
thought-provoking statements.

Although it is certainly better to exercise self-control than
to yield to all the appetites of the body, self-control is not
necessarily spiritually motivated. Some of the greatest dem-
onstrations of self-discipline today are seen in various cults
which do not even believe in the deity of Christ or salvation
by grace through faith. For the believer, his rule of life is not
a system of regulations but "Christ in you, the hope of glory"
(1:27). The power of Christ not only restrains the desires of
the flesh, but it also puts new, godly desires within us. Our
appetites, or wants, are changed.

Someone once approached D. L. Moody and said, "There is
something wrong with you, Mr. Moody. You do not believe in
the theater." "Oh," he said, "lady, you've got me wrong. I go
to the theater every time I want to." As she looked at him
quizzically, he went on to say, "But I want you to know I
don't want to." In other words, God had changed his
"wanter."

We experience a complete change when we trust Jesus
Christ as our personal Saviour. At that moment, God's sal-

vation is worked within us. We then work out that salvation so a lost world might see Christ in our lives (see Phil. 2:12,13). But it is important to realize that the Christ we have received as our Saviour is all sufficient.

Chapter 8

Let Christ Live Through You

As emphasized previously, the first two chapters of Colossians emphasize doctrine; the last two emphasize practice. The theme of the first two chapters is "Christ in You"; the theme in the last two chapters is "Let Christ Live Again." The first two chapters emphasize Christ's living in us; the last two, Christ's living through us.

It is the normal order in the New Testament to stress doctrine before practice. The way one lives is determined by what he believes. If there is an improper basis of belief, there can only be improper living. But proper beliefs are the groundwork for proper living.

Although doctrine is the basis for practice, it accomplishes little if the believer declares and defends the truth but fails to demonstrate it in his daily life. The Bible should not be taught for teaching's sake alone; it is to be taught so its truths can be lived out. The question that each of us who knows Christ as Saviour needs to ask himself is "How do I translate Bible knowledge into Christian living?" In pagan religions—both in Bible times and now—the worshiper bows to his idols, places an offering on the altar, then leaves to live the same as always. But the Christian faith presents an entirely new concept of religion. What we believe has a definite connection with the way we behave. For instance, what a man believes about death and the hereafter determines to a large degree how he lives now.

Our faith in Christ has brought about regeneration, as we have learned from Colossians 1 and 2. This means we are united to Christ in whom dwells the fullness of the Godhead bodily (2:9,10). Since we share Christ's life, His character should be seen in us.

It is not enough for Christ to be preeminent, or to be

supreme, in redemption, creation and the Church. He must also be supreme, or be Lord, in our lives. He desires that His supremacy over all things be clearly demonstrated through our lives.

It has been shown that in Christ's death we also died spiritually to sin, self, the Law and the world. But there was also a spiritual resurrection! As Christ rose physically from the grave, we also rose with Him spiritually. This is why Romans 6:13 tells us, "Neither yield ye your members as instruments of unrighteousness unto sin: but yield yourselves unto God, as those that are alive from the dead, and your members as instruments of righteousness unto God."

Since in Christ dwells all the fullness of the Godhead bodily, so in our union with Him we are filled, or made complete (see Col. 2:9,10). The last two chapters of Colossians show that the truth of the first two chapters supplies the genuine and adequate power for all that the believer needs. Because of our position in Christ, we have adequate power against any and all indulgence of the flesh, plus the possibility of holy living as we appropriate what Christ has made available to us. And it is important that the truths be appropriated in the way Christ has provided, not in the way prescribed by the false teachers. Thus, again we see that all right living necessarily springs from right doctrine.

Resurrection With Christ

As Paul began the section of his epistle on practice, he wrote: "If ye then be risen with Christ, seek those things which are above, where Christ sitteth on the right hand of God" (Col. 3:1).

Here again we are confronted with an "if," even as we were in Colossians 1:23. In the original language, this particular construction can indicate a simple condition, but it also can indicate an assumed reality. Because Paul was writing to believers, the word can be legitimately translated "since." The truths he presented would not apply to unbelievers, but to believers Paul was saying, "Since you have been raised with Christ, seek those things which are above."

Here we have the basis for the heavenly walk—one's resurrection with Christ. It is not a wish; it is a fact that is true of every person who has trusted Christ as his Saviour.

Each believer has been united with Christ, not only in His death but also in His resurrection. Paul said, "For if we had been planted together in the likeness of his death, we shall be also in the likeness of his resurrection" (Rom. 6:5).

The words "risen with" in Colossians 3:1 are translated from a single Greek word literally meaning "raised together" or "co-raised." This truth—even the same Greek word—is also stated in Ephesians 2:6: "And hath raised us up together, and made us sit together in heavenly places in Christ Jesus." The same word also appears in Colossians 2:12: "Buried with him in baptism, wherein also ye are risen with him through the faith of the operation of God, who hath raised him from the dead."

Christ's resurrection was a physical one. The believer's resurrection is a spiritual one. The one who trusts in the finished work of Christ for his salvation is raised from a state of spiritual death into that of spiritual life. This is the *potential* for all who would believe, and it becomes the *actual* experience of everyone who places faith in Christ as Saviour and Lord. Since this is the actual experience of everyone who has believed in Christ, the believer's walk, or manner of life, is also to be a heavenly one. Such a walk of the believer is not by sheer willpower; it is by His power.

It is wonderful to realize that, as believers, we live by the power of Christ's resurrection life. As we do this, we are letting Christ live again in the sense that He is living out His life through us. This is what Paul desired for the Ephesian believers, for he prayed that they might know "what is the exceeding greatness of his power to us-ward who believe, according to the working of his mighty power, which he wrought in Christ, when he raised him from the dead, and set him at his own right hand in the heavenly places" (Eph. 1:19,20). This ties in beautifully with Paul's statement in Colossians 1:27: "Christ in you, the hope of glory."

It must be remembered that we are not robots, operated by push buttons. We are beings with the power of choice, and we must decide to apply these truths to ourselves. God's wants us to surrender to Him as an act of faith. When we do this, God works on our behalf. This is not necessarily only a New Testament truth. The psalmist wrote: "Commit thy way unto the Lord; trust also in him; and he shall bring it to pass"

(Ps. 37:5). We have also frequently stressed Philippians 2:12 and Galatians 5:16 which indicate that we are to work out the salvation that has been worked within us and that we are to live by means of the Spirit.

Paul stressed to the believers in Colossae—and to us—that as a result of their standing in Christ they had a great responsibility to "seek those things which are above, where Christ sitteth on the right hand of God" (Col. 3:1).

Responsibility to Seek Things Above

Colossians 3:2 tells how this is to be done: "Set your affection on things above, not on things on the earth." The words "set your affection on" are translated from the common Greek word for "think on." Paul wanted the Colossians to think on those things that have heavenly origin rather than those things which have an earthly one. Another way of saying the same thing would be: "Apply your mind" to what is above.

The tense of the word involved indicates that one's thinking is to be constantly fixed on that which is above. It is not something that is to happen only once—or even occasionally. It is to be a continual process. When the believer rises from sleep, he should set his affection on heavenly things, and throughout the day he should discipline his mind to keep it fixed on things that count not only for time but also for eternity. Another way of expressing the same truth would be "Constantly give your heart to heavenly things."

This reveals to us that the way we "seek those things which are above" (v. 1) is by thinking "on things above" (v. 2). Some seem to seek heaven, but they do not seem to think heaven.

In his latter years, I recall that my father was thinking heaven almost constantly. Heaven was very precious and dear to him. I realize that, for the believer, this is more common as we get older. I am older now than my father was at his death, and I know from experience that, as the Lord becomes more precious, we think heaven more.

By itself, "seek" (v. 1) refers to a practical striving, whereas "set your affection" (v. 2) refers to the inward impulse and disposition. This is an attitude.

Remember, the things on earth are not in themselves sinful, but it is sinful to seek them and think on them in preference to the things that are above.

Illustration of Abraham and Lot

Two men in the Old Testament illustrate this truth very clearly. Abraham and Lot were both rich in this world's goods, but they had completely different attitudes toward their possessions. Abraham was heavenly minded, whereas Lot was earthly minded. This is seen from the information recorded in Genesis 13 when Abraham was known as "Abram." The Bible says, "And Abram was very rich in cattle, in silver, and in gold. And he went on his journeys from the south even to Beth-el, unto the place where his tent had been at the beginning, between Beth-el and Hai; unto the place of the altar, which he had made there at the first: and there Abram called on the name of the Lord" (vv. 2-4).

Notice what is said concerning Lot: "Lot also, which went with Abram, had flocks, and herds, and tents" (v. 5). Even though Lot may not have had as much as Abraham, it is apparent that Lot was rich as far as the standards of his time were concerned.

This created a problem between Abraham and Lot: "The land was not able to bear them, that they might dwell together: for their substance was great, so that they could not dwell together" (v. 6). In addition to their needing more land for their herds, Lot and Abraham were being forced to separate because of their servants' inability to get along with each other.

When it came time for them to separate, notice the attitude which Abraham had. He told Lot, "Is not the whole land before thee? separate thyself, I pray thee, from me: if thou wilt take the left hand, then I will go to the right; or if thou depart to the right hand, then I will go to the left" (v. 9). What a gracious and generous man Abraham was!

Being offered first choice, it is significant to see what Lot chose. "Lot lifted up his eyes, and beheld all the plain of Jordan, that it was well watered every where, before the Lord destroyed Sodom and Gomorrah, even as the garden of the Lord, like the land of Egypt, as thou comest unto Zoar. Then Lot chose him all the plain of Jordan; and Lot journeyed

east: and they separated themselves the one from the other"
(vv. 10,11).

Verses 12 and 13 summarize by stating, "Abram dwelled
in the land of Canaan, and Lot dwelled in the cities of the
plain, and pitched his tent toward Sodom. But the men of
Sodom were wicked and sinners before the Lord exceedingly." Thus, we see the lives of these two men moving down
different paths which indicate the attitudes they had toward
the things of this world.

It would seem that Abraham certainly came out second
best because of his unselfish spirit in letting Lot have first
choice. But God honors those who are unselfish and put Him
and others first. "The Lord said unto Abram, after that Lot
was separated from him, Lift up now thine eyes, and look
from the place where thou art northward, and southward,
and eastward, and westward: for all the land which thou
seest, to thee will I give it, and to thy seed for ever"
(vv. 14,15).

God told Abraham, "Arise, walk through the land in the
length of it and in the breadth of it; for I will give it unto thee"
(v. 17).

And how do you think Abraham responded when God
extended to him such great blessing? Here again we see
Abraham's attitude reflected, for he "removed his tent, and
came and dwelt in the plain of Mamre, which is in Hebron,
and built there an altar unto the Lord" (v. 18). He responded
by worshiping the Lord.

Lot eventually lost everything he owned as he had to flee
from Sodom and Gomorrah before God hailed fire and brim-
stone on them (see Gen. 19). The attitudes of these two men
cause us to realize that those who seek the things of this
world wind up empty handed. Some do not necessarily wind
up empty handed in this world, but they do in the world to
come. But many even lose everything in this world. It is
heartbreaking to think of what happened to Lot, but it is also
heartbreaking to think about so many present-day Christians who are more concerned about the things of time than
about the things of eternity. They have salvation, but they
give God very little place in their daily lives. Romans 12:1,2
exhorts us, "I beseech you therefore, brethren, by the mercies
of God, that ye present your bodies a living sacrifice, holy,

acceptable unto God, which is your reasonable service. And be not conformed to this world: but be ye transformed by the renewing of your mind, that ye may prove what is that good, and acceptable, and perfect, will of God."

The "renewing of your mind" (v. 2) relates to the truth emphasized in Colossians 3:2: "Set your affection on things above, not on things on the earth." Paul urged the Philippians: "Let this mind [way of thinking] be in you, which was also in Christ Jesus" (Phil. 2:5). The Lord Jesus Christ was unselfish because He gave up the glory which He had with the Father in order to come to this world to die for our sins. We are to have this kind of unselfish attitude by which we put more emphasis on eternal realities than on temporal ones.

When Paul urged believers to set their minds on things above rather than on things on the earth (Col. 3:2), he was asking for a clear-cut break with earthly, or material, things as far as our dependence on, and affection for, those things was concerned. Paul wanted believers to have minds that were separated unto God. Although we are *in* the world, we are not to be *of* the world.

Reasons for Paul's Exhortation

Having given the exhortation for believers to set their minds on things above, Paul gave four reasons for doing so. The exhortation is in Colossians 3:1,2, and the four reasons are in verses 3 and 4: "For ye are dead, and your life is hid with Christ in God. When Christ, who is our life, shall appear, then shall ye also appear with him in glory." The four reasons for Paul's exhortation were: (1) "For ye are dead"; (2) "your life is hid with Christ in God"; (3) "Christ, who is our life, shall appear"; (4) "then shall ye also appear with him in glory." Let us now consider each one of these significant reasons.

"For Ye Are Dead"

First, "for ye are dead" (Col. 3:3). Because the believer has died to self and the world with the Lord Jesus Christ and has been given a position in Christ where sin has no more claim on his life, the believer should seek the things which are above. Romans 6:6 says, "Knowing this, that our old man is

[was] crucified with him, that the body of sin might be destroyed, that henceforth we should not serve sin." Colossians 1:13 also emphasizes what God did for us at the time of salvation: "Who hath delivered us from the power of darkness, and hath translated us into the kingdom of his dear Son." This means that we can have victory over the old self, or sin nature, which would still like to control us. Having experienced the grace of God, our attitude should be the same as Paul's: "How shall we that are dead to sin, live any longer therein?" (Rom. 6:2).

"Your Life Is Hid With Christ"

A second reason for Paul's exhortation for believers to set their affection on things above is "Your life is hid with Christ in God" (Col. 3:3). This is a reference to the believer's spiritual life. Our spiritual life is really Christ's life. The word "hid" emphasizes that we are kept in Christ. A similar truth is emphasized by Paul in Galatians 2:20: "I am crucified with Christ: nevertheless I live; yet not I, but Christ liveth in me."

Since the believer's life "is hid with Christ in God" (Col. 3:3), the Christian cannot be touched or hurt by any evil power—originating with man or the Devil—apart from God's permission.

The believer's life is also a hidden life as far as the world is concerned. Because the world does not know Jesus Christ as Saviour, it does not have the capacity to understand the believer. The values and motives of the believer are misunderstood by people of the world, who live only by the five senses. The believer, however, because he has been translated into the kingdom of God's Son, lives by heavenly values and desires to do that which counts for eternity.

Jesus warned those of us who believe in Him as Saviour that the world would not be our friend: "If the world hate you, ye know that it hated me before it hated you. If ye were of the world, the world would love his own: but because ye are not of the world, but I have chosen you out of the world, therefore the world hateth you" (John 15:18,19). One of the key reasons the world does not understand the believer is because the believer lives by faith. Imagine what the people of Abraham's time thought of him as he lived by faith, as recorded in

Hebrews 11:9,10: "By faith he sojourned in the land of promise, as in a strange country, dwelling in tabernacles [tents] with Isaac and Jacob, the heirs with him of the same promise: for he looked for a city which hath foundations, whose builder and maker is God." Abraham certainly lived by a different value system than the people around him—he lived by faith, not by sight.

The fact that the believer's life is "hid with Christ in God" (Col. 3:3) emphasizes Christ's union, or oneness, with God. This is in line with the statement in 2:9: "For in him dwelleth all the fulness of the Godhead bodily." But the fact that our lives are hid with Christ in God also emphasizes our union with God in Christ, which is in agreement with 2:10: "And ye are complete in him."

"Christ, Who Is Our Life"

The third reason for Paul's exhortation to believers to be heavenly minded is seen from his statement "When Christ, who is our life, shall appear" (Col. 3:4). Notice especially the words "Christ, who is our life." It is not enough to say that our life is shared with Christ; rather, we must say that our spiritual life *is* the life of Christ. This is not to be toned down to mean that Christ is the possessor and the giver of this life; He Himself is the very essence of the Christian life.

One cannot have eternal life apart from having the Son of God Himself. This is especially emphasized in I John 5:11,12: "And this is the record, that God hath given to us eternal life, and this life is in his Son. He that hath the Son hath life; and he that hath not the Son of God hath not life."

So God's eternal life is not some heavenly substance that He shares with the sinner who trusts Christ as Saviour; it is the life of Christ Himself. It is "Christ in you, the hope of glory" (Col. 1:27). This great truth brought excitement to the Apostle Paul.

"Then Shall Ye Also Appear With Him"

The fourth reason Paul exhorted believers to think on those things which are above was "Then shall ye also appear with him in glory" (Col. 3:4). Because Christ's manifestation in His glory means our manifestation with Him, this is reason to think on those things which are above.

The Apostle John emphasized the same truth: "Beloved, now are we the sons of God, and it doth not yet appear what we shall be: but we know that, when he shall appear, we shall be like him; for we shall see him as he is. And every man that hath this hope in him purifieth himself, even as he is pure" (I John 3:2,3). The hope of being glorified with Christ does something to the believer; it causes him to live a purified life.

Paul reminded believers, "For our conversation [citizenship] is in heaven; from whence also we look for the Saviour, the Lord Jesus Christ" (Phil. 3:20). Since our home is in heaven, we ought to have a heavenly walk while on this earth. We are now not only assured of a position in Christ, but for the future we are assured of being glorified together with Him. Knowing and acting on the basis of these facts should make a difference in our lives.

Jesus said, "Where your treasure is, there will your heart be also" (Matt. 6:21). In a sense, we can say, "Where your home is, there will your affection be also." Our home is in heaven, and the more we are truly aware of this, the more we will be concerned about the things of heaven.

Do you know what it is to long for home? Occasionally I leave home for three or four days—sometimes as long as a week—to do concentrated study on a series of messages. Over the years I have found it helpful to do this in order to be away from the pressures of the office and the telephone. But when I am away, I get homesick—especially for my wife. So while I am gone, I call her several times just to talk with her.

The believer's real home is heaven, for he is seated "together in heavenly places in Christ Jesus" (Eph. 2:6). When we know this and act upon it as the basis of faith, our affection will be centered more and more in heaven.

The Application of Spiritual Principles

Having shown what the believer's position is in Christ and urging him to set his affection on things above, Paul then turned to the application of these spiritual principles (Col. 3:5-17). Verses 5-7 pronounce death on the sinful life. Paul said, "Mortify therefore your members which are upon the earth; fornication, uncleanness, inordinate affection, evil concupiscence, and covetousness, which is idolatry: for which things' sake the wrath of God cometh on the children of disobedience: in the which ye also walked some time, when ye lived in them."

"Mortify Your Members"

Here we see that our new life within (Christ) demands a new life without (our behavior). The Lord Jesus Christ wants to be far more than a ticket to heaven for us; He desires to produce new behavior in us. But in order for this to happen, we must act upon the fact that we have died to the sin nature and are very much alive in Him. When the sin nature appeals to us to see, hear and say the wrong things, we can say no to its appeal. This is the way we "mortify" it (v. 5), or put it to death. Instead, we can yield, or present, our eyes, ears and tongue to Jesus Christ to do those things which honor Him.

We "mortify" by putting to death, or depriving of power, or destroying the strength of, the flesh. Romans 8:13 says, "For if ye live after the flesh, ye shall die: but if ye through the Spirit do mortify the deeds of the body, ye shall live."

As believers we now have both the authority and the spiritual power to pronounce death to our "members which are upon the earth; fornication, uncleanness, inordinate affection, evil concupiscence, and covetousness" (Col. 3:5). Our need is to be "strong in the Lord, and in the power of his might" (Eph. 6:10). We also need to heed Paul's words in Romans 6:11: "Likewise reckon ye also yourselves to be dead indeed unto sin, but alive unto God through Jesus Christ our Lord." This may seem difficult, but remember the words of Philippians 4:13: "I can do all things through Christ which strengtheneth me."

The words of Colossians 3:5, "Mortify therefore your members which are upon the earth," imply a definite act of faith based on the authority of our union with Christ. The believer is to put to death those things that belong to his earthly nature. This can be done because it is a fact we have died with Christ.

Romans 6:11 reveals that we are not only to count ourselves as being "dead indeed unto sin" but we are also to count ourselves as being "alive unto God through Jesus Christ our Lord." This presents both a negative and a positive—death and life. It does not allow for a wishful, or a hopeful, attitude that something *might* happen. The Scriptures are speaking of facts here, and we are to stand firm in our position on the basis of these facts. James said, "He that wavereth is like a wave of the sea driven with the wind and tossed. For let not that man think that he shall receive any thing of the Lord" (James 1:6,7).

The believer is to put to death whatever belongs to his earthly nature; he is not to allow his members to be used in the service of sin. In Colossians 3:5 Paul named some of the sins which belong to the earthly life. They are sins that are characteristic of the children of disobedience: "Fornication, uncleanness, inordinate affection, evil concupiscence, and covetousness, which is idolatry." Paul further explained, "For which things' sake the wrath of God cometh on the children of disobedience" (v. 6). Paul reminded the Colossians of their past life when he said, "In the which ye also walked some time, when ye lived in them" (v. 7).

Let us not mislead any: A believer never becomes perfect in this life; so he is never completely free from sin. However, the characteristic of the believer is that he will not continue, or practice, sin even though he occasionally sins. The Bible says, "Whosoever is born of God doth not commit [practice] sin; for his seed remaineth in him: and he cannot sin, because he is born of God" (I John 3:9). This verse does not teach that a believer never sins; it teaches that he does not continue in sin, or habitually sin. The person who is habitually sinning indicates that he or she has never trusted Jesus Christ as Saviour and experienced a change of life. Although I had grown up in a Christian home, I came to the realization at the age of 20 that I had never personally trusted Jesus Christ as my Lord and Saviour, and that is why I had not experienced the change of life about which the Scriptures speak.

Sins of the Old Nature

Paul mentioned the particular sins that characterize the earthly nature. First, he referred to "fornication" (Col. 3:5). This refers to any illicit sexual act.

Second, Paul mentioned "uncleanness" (v. 5), which refers to impurity that is connected with loose living. This can refer to an impurity not only of the body but also of the mind. It is not sufficient just to get victory over using the body for impure purposes; one must also gain victory over the impurity of the mind. Although we cannot prevent a particular thought from coming to our minds, we can immediately ask the Lord to take over and control our minds so we do not continue to think unclean thoughts.

Third, Paul mentioned "inordinate affection" (v. 5), which refers to passion or sensual desires. Romans 1 comments about those with depraved passions: "Therefore God gave them over in the sinful desires of their hearts to sexual impurity for the degrading of their bodies with one another. They exchanged the truth of God for a lie, and worshiped and served created things rather than the Creator—who is forever praised. Amen. Because of this, God gave them over to shameful lusts. Even their women exchanged natural relations for unnatural ones. In the same way the men also abandoned natural relations with women and were inflamed with lust for one another. Men committed indecent acts with other men, and received in themselves the due penalty for their perversion. Furthermore, since they did not think it worthwhile to retain the knowledge of God, he gave them over to a depraved mind, to do what ought not to be done" (vv. 24-28, NIV).

In Colossians 3:5 "evil concupiscence" refers to evil, or wicked, cravings. They are evil, or unholy, desires.

Fourth, Paul referred to "covetousness" (v. 5), which is the desire to have more and more. It is an excessive desire for wealth. Paul called this idolatry because it relegates God to a secondary place. The sin of always wanting more—whether things or pleasures—is idolatry and brings the wrath of God on the unsaved. "For which things' sake the wrath of God cometh on the children of disobedience" (v. 6).

"Put Off . . . Put On"

Paul continued his emphasis on practice by telling believers to "put off" certain things and to "put on" others (Col. 3:8-14).

Paul said, "But now ye also put off all these; anger, wrath, malice, blasphemy, filthy communication out of your mouth. Lie not one to another, seeing that ye have put off the old man with his deeds; and have put on the new man, which is renewed in knowledge after the image of him that created him" (vv. 8-10).

The terminology "put off" and "put on" is the same as used in dressing and undressing. In this context, the emphasis is on changing clothes. The believer is to put off the filthy garments associated with the flesh and to put on the new garments that are associated with righteousness, or holiness.

Put Off Sin

In Christ, we have already put off the old man positionally. But it is important that we make this real in our personal experience. Putting away the uncleanness of the past was emphasized in Colossians 2:11: "In whom also ye are circumcised with the circumcision made without hands, in putting off the body of the sins of the flesh by the circumcision of Christ." I like the way one person has expressed this concept: "As you have put off the old man, now put off his clothes."

Positionally, God sees the believer in Christ. The old man has been crucified and is counted dead. So the believer is here exhorted to make it so in practical experience by reckoning, or counting, it true by a once-for-all act of faith.

In Colossians 3:5-7 the believer is urged to pronounce death on sensual sins. In verses 8-14 the believer is being asked to deal with social sins. Since the believer has put off the old man, he is now asked to put off those qualities which characterized the old man.

The putting off of these social sins is comparable to what Jesus did with His grave clothes at the resurrection. He left them behind because they were no longer needed. He had entered into a glorious resurrection life and was leaving behind all that characterized death. He put off the grave clothes as He entered the resurrection life in His glorified body.

So we also have been raised with Christ and have no need of our grave clothes. They represent the old life with its sinful deeds, but now we need to put on that which characterizes our new life in Christ. Just as Lazarus was bound in his grave clothes (John 11:44) when Jesus called him forth from the grave, so we are bound by sin in our unsaved state. But just as Jesus commanded Lazarus to be loosed from his grave clothes, so we—by faith in Christ—are loosed from the bondage of sin. But it is important that we recognize this to be a fact. We are to reckon this to be so because it is so. We can have abundant life only as we recognize what we have in Christ and live accordingly. By so doing, we practice our position in Christ (see Rom. 6).

In Colossians 3:8,9 notice the specific sins which Paul told believers to put off. "Anger" (v. 8) refers to an abiding, or habitual, anger that includes revenge. "Wrath" (v. 8) is similar to anger but especially refers to a sudden, violent outburst of anger.

"Malice" (v. 8) refers to an attitude of ill will toward another person; it is the desire to cause injury or to pay back what has been done.

"Blasphemy" (v. 8) refers to using words to slander others, or to tear them down. It is the act of being injurious to another person's good name. Malicious gossip fits in this category and is sin.

"Filthy communication" (v. 8) refers to foul speech with its coarse humor and obscene language.

Lying (v. 9) is the last sin mentioned in Paul's list. He clearly commanded, "Lie not one to another." Jesus Himself said that the Devil "is a liar, and the father of it" (John 8:44). Therefore, when one lies, he is cooperating with Satan, who is the father of lies; but when he speaks the truth, he is cooperating with the Holy Spirit, who is the Spirit of truth.

Whereas some make distinctions between white lies and black ones or little lies and big ones, God makes no such distinctions—believers are simply told "lie not one to another" (Col. 3:9). All of these things are to be put off because they characterize the old self.

Put On the New Man

In contrast to those things which are to be put off, some things need to be put on. Paul said, "And have put on the new man, which is renewed in knowledge after the image of him that created him" (Col. 3:10).

The new man is the regenerate man in whom Christ is formed. "Christ in you" (1:27) is the new nature. That believers are "partakers of the divine nature" is seen from II Peter 1:4.

In Colossians 3:10,11 Paul revealed three truths about those who have put on the new man. First, they have a divine nature. Each person who trusts Christ as Saviour has "put on the new man, which is renewed in knowledge after the image of him that created him" (v. 10). It is not just that a person wants a new nature—he has a new nature. We translate our position into daily living as we say yes to Christ and no to sin.

Second, those who have trusted Christ as Saviour also have a new unity: "Where there is neither Greek nor Jew, circumcision nor uncircumcision, Barbarian, Scythian, bond nor free" (v. 11). The new unity transcends all races, social positions, cultural differences—even economic and political status. Such distinctions belong to the old man, not to the new man. And because God makes no distinctions between the categories mentioned in verse 11, neither should we who know Jesus Christ as Saviour.

Third, those who have trusted Jesus Christ have a new relationship: "Christ is all, and in all" (v. 11). This is a new relationship where Christ is in absolute control. Is Christ in control of your life? Not just in control of something, but is He in control of all things? Is He truly "all, and in all"?

True deliverance from all that relates to the old self comes as we claim, by faith, our position in Christ. We need to make real in our own lives the truths stated in Ephesians 2:5,6: "Even when we were dead in sins, hath quickened us [made us alive] together with Christ, (by grace ye are saved;) and hath raised us up together, and made us sit together in heavenly places in Christ Jesus." We not only have Christ in us, but we are also positionally seated together with Him in the heavenlies.

Colossians 3:9,10 were exceedingly important verses for the Colossians, and they are for us too. Because they had put off the old man positionally in Christ, Paul wanted them to make it so in their personal experience. And because they had put on the new man positionally in Christ, Paul wanted them to also make this so in personal experience.

The position which the believer has in Christ became his instantaneously when he trusted Christ as Saviour. But making this position real in daily experience is a process that lasts a lifetime. That is why verse 10 says the new man "is renewed in knowledge after the image of him that created him." As someone has said, "The crisis of salvation leads to the process of sanctification." "The process of sanctification" means becoming more like Jesus Christ. This process is seen in Ephesians 2:10: "For we are his workmanship, created in Christ Jesus unto good works, which God hath before ordained that we should walk in them."

The process is also seen in Romans 8:28: "We know that all things work together for good to them that love God, to them who are the called according to his purpose." Although this verse is known to so many believers, few seem to realize that the purpose is stated in the next verse: "For whom he did foreknow, he also did predestinate to be conformed to the image of his Son, that he might be the firstborn among many brethren" (v. 29). God's purpose in working all things together for our good is that we might be conformed to the image of His Son. And how is this done? By reading the Word of God and applying its truths to our lives. This is seen from II Corinthians 3:18: "But we all, with open face beholding as in a glass the glory of the Lord, are changed into the same image from glory to glory, even as by the Spirit of the Lord."

Warren W. Wiersbe, Back to the Bible's associate Bible teacher, has stated this truth so well: "When the Child of God looks into the Word of God and sees the Son of God, he is changed by the Spirit of God into the Image of God for the Glory of God."

Since the believer has once and for all put on the new man, he is constantly being "renewed in knowledge after the image of him that created him" (Col. 3:10). The believer experiences a change in the quality of his life as he becomes more like Jesus Christ. In other words, others will increasingly see Christ in our lives as we grow in our knowledge of Him. The better we get to know Christ, the more we become like Him. This was why Paul had the burning desire to know Christ better (see Phil. 3:10).

After Paul's statements to the Colossians about putting off the things of the old man and putting on the things of the new, he explained how to know Christ and grow in Him. The first thing we must know is that Christ is the center, the circumference and everything in between that pertains to the new man. "Christ is all, and in all" (Col. 3:11). Christ occupies the whole sphere of life and permeates all its development. In fact, this emphasis is what the entire letter to the Colossians is all about (see 1:18; 2:3,9,10).

Walking in the Newness of Life

Paul continued to emphasize to the Colossians that they should practice their position in Christ. Colossians 3:12-17 might well be called "Walking in the Newness of Life." This is borrowing a phrase from Romans 6:4: "Therefore we are buried with him by baptism into death: that like as Christ was raised up from the dead by the glory of the Father, even so we also should walk in newness of life." The provisions for such a walk include the motivating power, or enablement, for it. This motivating power is provided totally in Christ.

Some of the various graces of the new life are given in verses 12-17. They reveal what God has made available for us to victoriously live the Christian life. For instance, some of the graces mentioned are "charity [love]" (v. 14), "the peace of God" (v. 15), "the word of Christ" (v. 16). He also provided the use of the "name of the Lord Jesus" (v. 17) for the necessary authority against all evil, especially the Evil One.

As one reads verses 8-17, he becomes aware that Paul did not just emphasize the negative aspects of the Christian life. Paul dealt with the negative aspects—what should be put off (vv. 8,9), but he also emphasized the positive aspects—what should be put on (vv. 10-17). The enablement to do all of this comes from God Himself. As long as we live in this sinful world, in the body of death, with the old nature present, we must constantly apply, by faith, the graces that God supplies.

Do not be mistaken, the Christian life can be perplexing and frustrating as one seeks to do what he knows is right. Romans 7 records the frustration Paul went through as he found himself occasionally doing what he knew he should not do and not doing what he knew he should do. Finally, he exclaimed, "What a wretched man I am! Who will rescue me from this body of death?" (v. 24, NIV). Paul answered his own question in the following verse: "Thanks be to God— through Jesus Christ our Lord!" (v. 25, NIV). Paul continued his answer, especially in 8:2-4: "Through Christ Jesus the law of the Spirit of life set me free from the law of sin and death. For what the law was powerless to do in that it was weakened by the sinful nature, God did by sending his own Son in the likeness of sinful man to be a sin offering. And so he condemned sin in sinful man, in order that the righteous requirements of the law might be fully met in us, who do not live according to the sinful nature but according to the Spirit" (NIV).

In Colossians 3:12-17 we see both God's part and our part in the Christian life. By the power of the Holy Spirit, when we were born again, God enabled us to both put off the old and put on the new. This is an accomplished fact as far as God is concerned. Now, by the same Holy Spirit who indwells us, God provides all that is essential for putting off the old man experientially and putting on the new man experientially. Second Peter 1:3 tells what God has made available to us: "His divine power has given us everything we need for life and godliness through our knowledge of him who called us by his own glory and goodness" (NIV).

Colossians 3:12 says, "Put on therefore, as the elect of God, holy and beloved, bowels of mercies, kindness, humbleness of mind, meekness, longsuffering." Notice the three words that Paul used to describe believers: "elect . . . holy and beloved." From verse 13 we could add the word "forgiven" from the phrase "even as Christ forgave you."

The word "elect" means "chosen." God chose believers for a particular purpose—that He might demonstrate something very special in them and through them. "Holy" means "set apart." Being set apart involves a twofold action—turning from the world and turning to the Lord. We have stated this truth before as putting off the things of the world and putting on the things that characterize the new man. This is the least we can do because we have been bought with a price. Paul emphasized the matter of separation from the world and unto God in I Corinthians 6 and concluded by saying, "Do you not know that your body is a temple of the Holy Spirit, who is in you, whom you have received from God? You are not your own; you were bought at a price. Therefore honor God with your body" (vv. 19,20, NIV). Our bodies are God's precious possessions, and they are indwelt by the Holy Spirit if we have trusted Jesus Christ as personal Saviour.

Something that is set apart is to be used for what it is intended. For instance, a church sanctuary is set apart for worship—not as a game room for children to run around in. We use it for its intended purpose when we worship there.

The vows of a wedding ceremony also illustrate what happens when we are spiritually set apart. Each person vows to set himself apart from all others and give himself to the one he is marrying. Spiritual separation is being set apart from the world unto God.

Paul also referred to the Colossian believers as "beloved" (Col. 3:12) or literally "having been loved." That is, God has set His love upon us. This kind of love is what is commonly referred to as *agape;* in fact, the word used here comes from the same basic root. This is a giving kind of love, which forgets itself and sacrifices for others. This is evident from John 3:16: "God so loved . . . that he gave."

This special kind of God's love is also emphasized in Romans 8:35-39: "Who shall separate us from the love of Christ? Shall trouble or hardship or persecution or famine or nakedness or danger or sword? As it is written: 'For your sake we face death all day long; we are considered as sheep to be slaughtered.' No, in all these things we are more than conquerors through him who loved us. For I am convinced that neither death nor life, neither angels nor demons, neither the present nor the future, nor any powers, neither height nor depth, nor anything else in all creation, will be able to separate us from the love of God that is in Christ Jesus our Lord" (NIV).

As indicated previously, the fourth characteristic of believers is seen from Colossians 3:13: "Even as Christ forgave you." Have you thought about the fact that believers are only forgiven sinners? When we forget this, we become hard on others and unloving in our attitudes. How wonderful it is to have the promise of God: "Their sins and iniquities will I remember no more" (Heb. 10:17).

Mercy

Because believers are elect, holy, beloved (Col. 3:12) and forgiven (v. 13), there are eight qualities that they are urged to put on. First, "bowels of mercies" (v. 12). That is, a believer is to clothe himself with tender feelings of compassion toward others. This is not to be something one turns on and off like an electric light or radio, but it is to be the constant attitude of the heart. Because the believer is indwelt by God Himself, this quality is a characteristic of God that should be seen through his life. Lamentations 3:22,23 says, "It is of the Lord's mercies that we are not consumed, because his compassions fail not. They are new every morning: great is thy faithfulness." God never deviates from having a compassionate heart, and neither should we who know Him as Saviour.

Kindness

Second, the believer is to put on "kindness" (Col. 3:12). This refers to a gentle, gracious disposition. When I think of this quality, a particular godly leader comes to mind. Years ago another leader in the area did him much harm and sought to ruin his reputation. In a board meeting with this godly leader some of us expressed concern about what this other person was doing to him. This godly leader then made a statement I shall never forget: "I have determined in my heart to show love and kindness toward this Christian leader with all that I have." And he did. This is what kindness is all about.

A biblical illustration of showing kindness is seen from the life of David. The former king, Saul, had despised David and sought to kill him several times. But David never took advantage of Saul; in fact, Saul's son Jonathan became his closest friend. After the deaths of Saul and Jonathan, David asked, "Is there yet any that is left of the house of Saul, that I may shew him kindness for Jonathan's sake?" (II Sam. 9:1). It was then brought to David's attention that Jonathan had a crippled son, Mephibosheth (v. 3). David sent for Mephibosheth, and II Samuel 9 concludes by saying, "So Mephibosheth dwelt in Jerusalem: for he did eat continually at the king's table; and was lame on both his feet" (v. 13). In addition to providing for Mephibosheth continually, David also restored to him the land that had been confiscated from Saul. This was true kindness in action.

Humility

The third quality the believer is to put on is "humbleness of mind" (Col. 3:12). This means that the believer is to have a proper opinion of himself. It involves a modesty, or lowliness of thinking. I especially like the way Paul stated it in Romans 12:3, as translated in *The Amplified Bible:* "For by the grace (unmerited favor of God) given to me I warn every one among you not to estimate and think of himself more highly than he ought—not to have an exaggerated opinion of his own importance; but to rate his ability with sober judgment, each according to the degree of faith apportioned by God to him." Arthur S. Way paraphrases this same verse: "Do not be uplifted with unjustifiable notions of your importance. Let your thoughts tend to sober views."

The way one thinks is tremendously important in the Christian life. This is why Romans 12:16 says, "Be of the same mind one toward another. Mind not high things, but condescend to men of low estate. Be not wise in your own conceits." Or as we have already seen in Colossians 3:2: "Set your affection [mind] on things above, not on things on the earth." Paul told the believers in Philippi, "Fulfil ye my joy, that ye be likeminded, having the same love, being of one accord, of one mind. Let nothing be done through strife or vainglory; but in lowliness of mind let each esteem other better than themselves" (Phil. 2:2,3). All of these verses add up to: Others first, not self.

Meekness

The fourth quality that believers are to put on is "meekness" (Col. 3:12). Notice that the word is "meekness" not "weakness." The person who is meek is one who has the power of self-control and is slow to resent wrongs done to him. Such a person does not contemplate revenge.

The Greek word translated "meekness" was used in the first century to refer to a wild horse that had been tamed. It is strength under control.

The one who is meek is one who accepts God's dealings with him as good; therefore, he does not resist. There must first be a meekness toward God, but there must also be a meekness toward one's fellowmen, who may do evil toward the believer.

It is not difficult to find biblical illustrations of what the meek person is like. Moses was such a person. Numbers 12:3 says, "Now the man Moses was very meek, above all the men which were upon the face of the earth." Moses certainly had strength under control. When there were uprisings against him, such as when his brother and sister complained about his authority over them, Moses did not say a word (see Num. 12). Instead, God quickly spoke in Moses' behalf and made it clear to Aaron and Miriam that He had chosen to speak through Moses. God very emphatically let Aaron and Miriam know that if He chose to speak through anyone else, He would let that person know. Because of their boldness in speaking against God and His servant, Miriam was struck with leprosy, and Aaron appealed to Moses to do something about it.

Even in this we see the meekness of Moses, for even though Miriam had spoken against him, he asked the Lord in her behalf, "Heal her now, O God, I beseech thee" (v. 13). God promised to do so, but only after she had spent seven days outside the camp in seclusion because of her uncleanness.

Many other examples could be given from Moses' life which reveal he did not seek to defend himself when others spoke against him. Instead, he let God deal with the people, and then Moses characteristically prayed for them.

The Lord Jesus Christ is the supreme example of meekness. The Bible says of Him, "Who, when he was reviled, reviled not again; when he suffered, he threatened not; but committed himself to him that judgeth righteously" (I Pet. 2:23). This is also what we need to do when we are maligned. We need to commit ourselves to the Lord who is the righteous judge and let Him take care of the problems and people who trouble us. And count on this: If you are taking a stand for the Lord, some will talk against you.

The psalmist said, "Commit thy way unto the Lord; trust also in him; and he shall bring it to pass. And he shall bring forth thy righteousness as the light, and thy judgment as the noonday" (Ps. 37:5,6). I have relied on this promise hundreds of times.

Concerning the meekness of Christ, note how He described Himself: "Come unto me, all ye that labour and are heavy laden, and I will give you rest. Take my yoke upon you, and learn of me; for I am meek and lowly in heart: and ye shall find rest unto your souls" (Matt. 11:28,29).

Long-suffering

The fifth quality which Paul said should be put on by the believer is "longsuffering" (Col. 3:12). To have long-suffering means one is able to suffer long. Some are short tempered, but this is the one who is long tempered. This quality is known as patience when it relates to people. It is important that the believer not lose his temper when he is ill-treated by others. It is a characteristic of the old self to be short tempered; it should be a characteristic of the new self to be long tempered.

If you get worked up on the inside, go to God and pour out your heart. This will keep you from pouring out your bad feelings toward others. Apply Psalm 37:5,6 as already quoted.

Forbearance and Forgiveness

The sixth quality which Paul urged believers to put on was "forbearing one another" (Col. 3:13). The word translated "forbearing" also means "to put up with" or "endure."

The last three qualities we have examined—meekness, long-suffering and forbearing one another—closely relate to the quality that follows: "Forgiving one another" (v. 13).

It is not enough to be meek and take no offense. It is not enough to hold one's temper in check. It is not enough to endure. We must also forgive. If we harbor ill feelings and grudges in our hearts, this will result in malice and even greater sins. We need to be very careful in this regard. It is important that we forgive others when they have ill-treated us.

"But," someone may say, "you don't understand what all this person has done to me." That is true, but do you understand all that we did to Christ? Yet He forgave us. And that is the point Paul made in verse 13: "Forgiving one another, if any man have a quarrel against any: even as Christ forgave you, so also do ye." And this same Christ now indwells us to live out His life through us. The qualities that Paul mentioned for the Christian to put on are simply the qualities of the life of Christ. When we let Him have His way in our lives, these characteristics will be evident in us.

Love

The eighth quality which Paul said Christians should put on is "charity [love]" (Col. 3:14). Notice Paul's full statement in this regard: "And above all these things put on charity, which is the bond of perfectness [completeness]."

The robe of the Eastern man was held together by a girdle, which was put on last over all clothing. The girdle held everything together. In this regard, love serves as the girdle. Paul said, "And above all," which is literally, "and over all." Love is the quality that holds all of the other graces together. The Love Chapter of the Bible is I Corinthians 13. I am especially impressed by the way a portion of this chapter is translated in *The Amplified Bible:* "Love endures long and is patient and kind; love never is envious nor boils over with jealousy; is not boastful or vainglorious, does not display itself haughtily. It is not conceited—arrogant and inflated with pride; it is not rude (unmannerly), and does not act unbecomingly. Love [God's love in us] does not insist on its own rights or its own way, for it is not self-seeking; it is not touchy or fretful or resentful; it takes no account of the evil done to it—pays no attention to a suffered wrong. It does not rejoice at injustice and unrighteousness, but rejoices when right and truth prevail. Love bears up under anything and everything that comes, is ever ready to believe the best of every person, its hopes are fadeless under all circumstances and it endures everything [without weakening]. Love never fails—never fades out or becomes obsolete or comes to an end" (vv. 4-8).

As we have considered the qualities which Paul said the believer should put on, have you noticed how these closely parallel the fruit of the Spirit mentioned in Galatians 5:22,23? There, too, we find that "love" seems to be the prominent quality. These verses state, "But the fruit of the Spirit is love, joy, peace, longsuffering, gentleness, goodness, faith, meekness, temperance."

The note of explanation in *The Scofield Reference Bible* concerning these verses is especially significant: "Christian character is not mere moral or legal correctness, but the possession and manifestation of nine graces: love, joy, peace—character as an inward state; longsuffering, gentleness, goodness—character in expression toward man; faith, meekness, temperance—character in expression toward God. Taken together they present a moral portrait of Christ, and may be taken as the apostle's explanation of Gal. 2.20, 'Not I, but Christ,' and as a definition of 'fruit' in John 15.1-8. This character is possible because of the believer's vital union to Christ (John 15.5; 1 Cor. 12.12,13), and is wholly the fruit of the Spirit in those believers who are yielded to Him (Gal. 5.22,23)" (p. 1247).

From Galatians 5:22,23 and Colossians 3:14 it is possible to see that the quality of love may be regarded as the outer garment that holds all else together. In Colossians 3:14, Paul described this love as "the bond of perfectness." The word translated "perfectness" means "completeness" or "that which has been perfected." It is that which has reached its goal. As one commentator states it, love is "the power, which unites and holds together all those graces and virtues, which together make up perfection" (J. B. Lightfoot).

Peace of God

Moving on from the qualities the believer should put on, Paul exhorted, "Let the peace of God rule in your hearts, to the which also ye are called in one body; and be ye thankful" (Col. 3:15). The peace of God is the tranquillity of heart, or a state of calm and quiet freedom from disturbing thoughts and emotions. The believer is to be free from agitation or disturbance, for the peace of God will relieve his mental tension and anxiety.

As believers, we have peace *with* God as a result of accepting Christ as Saviour. Romans 5:1 says, "Therefore being justified by faith, we have peace with God through our Lord Jesus Christ." On the other hand, we experience the peace *of* God in our soul as we walk in the will of God. No doubt this is why Paul constantly prayed for the Colossians that they "might be filled with the knowledge of his will in all wisdom and spiritual understanding" (Col. 1:9).

An important question arises at this point: How can a believer know when he is doing the will of God? Colossians 3:15 is one of the best answers. Of course, if we are dealing with something that the Bible has clearly spoken for or against, we need to obey. However, there are many things we face which the Bible has not spoken on, such as what business we should be involved in, what school we should attend or what church we should choose. In any area where the Bible has not spoken clearly for or against, we are to let the peace of God rule in our hearts. This presupposes that the believer wishes to do what pleases Christ. That being the case, the believer can count on God to give an inner peace as an assurance of His will, or He will withhold peace as an indication it is not pleasing to Him.

The Greek word translated "rule" in Colossians 3:15 is similar in meaning to the word "umpire." Thus, we are to let the peace of God call the decisions in our hearts when we are dealing with those areas about which the Scriptures have not definitely spoken.

This same "peace of God" is referred to in Philippians 4:6,7: "Do not be anxious about anything, but in everything, by prayer and petition, with thanksgiving, present your requests to God. And the peace of God, which transcends all understanding, will guard your hearts and your minds in Christ Jesus" (NIV).

Although the peace of God is primarily related to the individual believer, it is important, as we labor together with others, that we experience the peace of God as a group. If we are to have an effective group, the individuals have to be at peace with each other. If individually the peace of God is being experienced, it will also be experienced as a group.

The Board of Trustees of Back to the Bible has experienced unusual harmony and the peace of God over the years. In fact, we have an unwritten rule that we do not take action unless a decision is unanimous. It is not that we could not take action, but we choose not to do so unless there is complete harmony and total agreement in the group. We want God's peace to act as our umpire in the many important decisions we make. If even one person does not have peace about the decision, the rest of us believe it needs to be considered further.

In any group, if some individuals are not experiencing the peace of God personally, there will be disunity and incompatibility in the group.

Tests of Peace

We must beware of false peace. Some who do wrong may have a peace about it, but it does not come from God. As someone has said, "Peace of heart alone is not always the peace of God."

A significant test to apply to determine the origin of the peace is this: If I have peace in my heart about a matter, do I also have peace with others in the Body of Christ concerning it? Understandably, not everyone will agree on any single issue, but if only the person himself thinks he is right, he has reason to question his decision. If we are out of the will of God, we will bring discord and disharmony to the Body of true believers. I realize the difficulty in assessing who is a true believer, especially in a group situation. Sometimes those who are part of the group do not evidence salvation themselves. Other times, some may clearly evidence salvation but give little evidence of mature judgment in things related to the Christian life.

One of the best safeguards against a false peace is simply making sure that you have the desire to please Jesus Christ in all that you do. If it is your concern "that in all things he might have the preeminence" (Col. 1:18), you can trust Him to bring conviction and a lack of peace when your life is not honoring to Him.

Another way to check out the genuineness of the peace is to evaluate whether or not you are heeding the last part of Colossians 3:15: "And be ye thankful." When there is peace of God in the heart, there will be thanksgiving in the heart. A Christian out of God's will is never filled with true praise to God.

Example of David

David provides an outstanding example of this truth. He had committed immorality with Bathsheba and had been instrumental in bringing about the death of her husband so he could have her. Later, he confessed his sin to God, but Psalm 32 records the agony through which he went before he confessed his sin. David said, "When I kept silent about my sin, my body wasted away through my groaning all day long. For day and night Thy hand was heavy upon me; my vitality was drained away as with the fever-heat of summer. I acknowledged my sin to Thee, and my iniquity I did not hide; I said, 'I will confess my transgressions to the Lord'; and Thou didst forgive the guilt of my sin" (vv. 3-5, NASB).

Psalm 51 is the record of David's confession itself. David prayed, "Purge me with hyssop, and I shall be clean: wash me, and I shall be whiter than snow. Make me to hear joy and gladness; that the bones which thou hast broken may rejoice" (vv. 7,8). David was unable to get along even with himself. His life was a mess, and he referred to himself as having broken bones.

Further, David prayed, "Restore unto me the joy of thy salvation; and uphold me with thy free spirit. Then will I teach transgressors thy ways; and sinners shall be converted unto thee" (vv. 12,13). David experienced the agony of being out of the will of God. The terrible feelings he experienced proved he had no peace whatever.

Word of God

In Colossians 3:16 Paul gave another important key to help one assess whether or not his peace was truly the peace of God: "Let the word of Christ dwell in you richly in all wisdom." The word refers to the message, or content, of God's revelation. The Bible is the written Word of God, or of Jesus Christ. And His Word is to guide us in our lives by giving us wisdom.

Many times when I have had important decisions to make—sometimes related to family affairs, other times related to the Back to the Bible ministry—I have found that the only thing I could do was to seclude myself with the Word of God and seek His will. I endeavored to get away from the usual pressures of life so I could give myself unreservedly to the Word of God so that I could check out with the Lord what His will was concerning this special situation. And I have discovered by personal experience that peace comes by the Word of God, as we "let the word of Christ dwell in [us] richly in all wisdom" (v. 16).

God always works through His Word, never apart from it. Even Paul's further instructions in Colossians 3:16 relate to basing everything on the Word: "Teaching and admonishing one another in psalms and hymns and spiritual songs, singing with grace in your hearts to the Lord."

Notice the special attention drawn to the Psalms. I would encourage you to read the Psalms so they might minister to your life. Especially notice the longest psalm of all—Psalm 119. This psalm particularly emphasizes the Word of God. I encourage you to use this psalm as a basis for devotional times to think through the importance of the Word of God to us. Let me single out a few verses that I think are especially significant in this regard: "Wherewithal shall a young man cleanse his way? by taking heed thereto according to thy word." "Thy word have I hid in mine heart, that I might not sin against thee." "I will never forget thy precepts: for with them thou hast quickened [made alive] me." "Thy word is a lamp unto my feet, and a light unto my path." "The entrance of thy words giveth light; it giveth understanding unto the simple." "Order my steps in thy word: and let not any iniquity have dominion over me" (vv. 9,11,93,105,130,133).

The Word is so important that I believe it can accurately be said that all who have ever accomplished great things, as far as God is concerned, have been people of the Word. They have been mighty in the Scriptures. Others think they have made a great splash in this life, but if it has not been based on the Word of God, it amounts to little.

We see how important the Word is from what Paul admonished Timothy: "I charge thee therefore before God, and the Lord Jesus Christ, who shall judge the quick [living] and the dead at his appearing and his kingdom; preach the word; be instant in season, out of season; reprove, rebuke, exhort with all longsuffering and doctrine" (II Tim. 4:1,2). Paul was exhorting Timothy to use the Word of God as it was intended to be used. Previously, Paul had said, "All scripture is given by inspiration of God, and is profitable for doctrine, for reproof, for correction, for instruction in righteousness: that the man of God may be perfect [mature], throughly furnished unto all good works" (3:16,17).

The importance of the Word of God is also seen from the words of Christ as He prayed to the Father: "Sanctify them through thy truth: thy word is truth" (John 17:17). Jesus also said, "Heaven and earth shall pass away: but my words shall not pass away" (Luke 21:33).

In Old Testament times, a famine of desiring to hear the
Word of God was prophesied: "Behold, the days come, saith
the Lord God, that I will send a famine in the land, not a
famine of bread, nor a thirst for water, but of hearing the
words of the Lord" (Amos 8:11). One certainly wonders if
that prophecy is not being fulfilled today. Not only are there
many liberal theologians who care little for the Word of God,
but also there are many in our Bible-believing churches who
do not seem to really desire an exposition of the Word of God.
It is more interesting to the masses to hear current issues
discussed than to think carefully about what God has said in
His Word. But if we are not concentrating on what the Word
of God says, it will not be long until the church is only a
meeting place for a religious club, not for believers whose
hearts are hungry to hear what God has said.

It is not enough to be taught the truth; we must possess it
as a present, personal experience. In proportion to how much
we meditate on God's Word and fill our minds with its truths,
we will have the power needed for victory and the means of
blessing. Everything in the Christian life is in one way or
another associated with the Word of God. That is why Satan
battles us so much concerning our being in the Word of God.
Satan realizes the Word is the basis for spiritual victory; so
he can most easily defeat us by keeping us out of the Word.

Notice that Colossians 3:16 commands believers to let the
word of Christ "dwell" in their hearts. The word translated
"dwell" means to "live" or "to dwell in." It has to do with
being at home. The Word will transform our lives if we just
permit it to be at home in us. Is the Word of God at home in
your life? Do you give it unrestricted liberty in your life?
Each of us who knows Christ as Saviour should desire that
the Word have an "at homeness" in us.

We realize we are growing in our relationship with the
Lord as we yearn for and love the Word of God more. Let us
keep returning to the Word of God to feed our own souls and
to determine the course we should take to honor the Lord.

Jesus Himself told us the results we could expect when we
give the Word a proper dwelling place in our hearts: "If ye
abide in me, and my words abide in you, ye shall ask what ye
will, and it shall be done unto you" (John 15:7). So it is

important that we "let the word of Christ dwell in [us]
richly" (Col. 3:16).

The word translated "richly" in Colossians 3:16 can also
have the meaning of "abundantly." We need to not only
yield to the Word of God but also to have a good knowledge of
it. This is important because the Holy Spirit always uses the
Word of God to search our hearts and to guide our lives.

Many people write or call Back to the Bible asking us to
pray for them. Many of these say something such as, "Please
pray for me that I might know the will of God." Of course, we
are always willing to pray for such people, but we endeavor
to point out that prayer alone is not sufficient in finding
God's will—one must also be immersed in the Word of God.
All of us who know Christ as Saviour need to realize that
unless we get into the Word of God, our praying accomplishes very little—if anything—in discovering God's will.
Praying is our talking to God; reading the Word allows God
to talk to us.

The Holy Spirit's language is the Word of God. That is why
it is important for each of us to answer: Is the Word of God
really at home in my life? My appeal to you is the same as
Paul made to the Colossian believers: "Let the word of Christ
dwell in you richly in all wisdom" (v. 16). Do you take time to
read the Word of God? Do you take time to study it; that is, do
you seek to master its contents? And beyond this, do you take
time to meditate on the Word of God?

In my devotional time each day I read until I gain something for my soul. Sometimes I read several chapters. Other
times I read only one verse because the content in it so meets
my need for that day that I spend my time meditating only
on it.

Memorizing the Word of God is an aid to meditating on it.
As we memorize it, we become more conscious of the precise
details of the Word, and we have it available to us to think
about even when we do not have a Bible available. Our goal
should be to apply to our lives what we gain in knowledge
and understanding. Our Bible study should produce a
change in our lives.

Notice from Paul's comment that the Word of Christ is to
dwell in us richly "in all wisdom; teaching and admonishing
one another in psalms and hymns and spiritual songs"

(v. 16). The words "teaching and admonishing" have the force of imperatives; that is, Paul was commanding believers to teach and admonish each other. The meaning of teaching is self-evident, although it might be helpful to emphasize again that what we are to teach is the Word of God. It is not just our own ideas or what someone else has said but the Word of God. The word "admonishing" means "warning"; in fact, the same Greek word translated "admonishing" here is translated "warning" in Colossians 1:28: "Whom we preach, warning every man, and teaching every man in all wisdom." So we are to warn, or exhort, others in the Word of God. We have already drawn attention to Paul's comments to Timothy about the importance of the Word of God and the urgency of proclaiming it while people will still listen (see II Tim. 3:16—4:2).

Notice that our teaching and admonishing is to be done "in psalms and hymns and spiritual songs" (Col. 3:16). There is a great poverty of proper Bible teaching in many churches today. This could be contributing to the fact that there are so many unscriptural and unspiritual songs today. Great songs of the faith come out of a rich Bible knowledge and a deep Christian experience.

In regard to writing music that reflects the riches of God's Word, I cannot help but think of Eugene L. Clark. For years he was actively involved with Back to the Bible's music. Then he became bedfast and unable to see. Yet in his arthritically crippled state he produced music that reflects the glory of God's Word. One of his greatest songs, in my opinion, is "Nothing Is Impossible." The message of this song was derived from the Scriptures as well as from personal experience. The song has had a worldwide distribution and has moved thousands to think on the wonderful truths of the Word of God. This is what Christian music should be and what it should bring about in the lives of its listeners.

Paul's use of the word "psalms" in Colossians 3:16 refers to what we know as the Book of Psalms. These were sung in Bible times, for the word "psalms" even means "songs." They were usually accompanied with stringed instruments. Some still sing them, but whether they are sung or not, they can be meditated on by all.

The first year we were in Lincoln we lived in a little house in which I had a very small study. If I wanted to have a really private place for prayer, I would go to the basement, which had a cement floor. There I arranged a bench, put a gunny sack down for a carpet and prayed. I distinctly remember doing something for my devotions that year that was one of the best things I have ever done. I prayed through every psalm on my knees. I made the statements of the psalms my statements of prayer to God as I praised Him. May I suggest that you endeavor to pray through the Psalms? I think you will find it a special blessing also.

Paul's use of the word "hymns" (v. 16) refers to songs of praise to God. These, of course, would be written by believers, for only they would know the Word of God and would have a desire to express true praise to God.

The words "spiritual songs" (v. 16) refer to any song that has a spiritual message. Whereas hymns would be especially directed to God, spiritual songs could be directed to fellow believers as well as to God. Spiritual songs would reflect the personal experiences of believers, which could be edifying to others. But in order for psalms, hymns and spiritual songs to be meaningful to us, the Word of God must be dwelling in us richly.

Paul also instructed that the different forms of songs be sung in a particular way: "Singing with grace in your hearts to the Lord" (v. 16). This is not a demonstration of human talent but a demonstration of God's grace in one's heart. In Philippi Paul and Silas were beaten and cast in prison. In spite of the fact that their backs were lacerated and they probably sat on the floor with their feet in stocks, their hearts were filled with singing. "At midnight Paul and Silas prayed, and sang praises unto God" (Acts 16:25). Read Acts 16 to see all that took place as God moved miraculously to deliver Paul and Silas from that prison and to bring about the salvation of the jailer and his household. Think of how God must have been pleased to hear Paul and Silas singing praises to Him in the midst of their physical agony.

In Colossians 3:16 Paul was especially concerned that singing be done "with grace in your hearts to the Lord." This is in contrast to some of the religious music one hears today. It seems as if much of the music performed today is for the display of one's voice or a demonstration of various musical

techniques. However, according to the Scriptures, the singing should always be God-centered, for it is to be "to the
Lord" (v. 16).

As one compares Colossians 3:16-19 with Ephesians 5:18-
22, he discovers that being filled with the Word of God produces the same blessings as being filled with the Spirit. So to
be filled with the Spirit means that we are filled, or controlled, by the Holy Spirit as He uses the Word of God in our
lives. In these passages we find that to be filled with the
Spirit and to be filled with the Word cause a person to be
joyful, thankful and submissive.

In the Name of Jesus

Colossians 3:17 serves as a summary statement to this
portion of Paul's letter to the Colossians: "Whatsoever ye do
in word or deed, do all in the name of the Lord Jesus, giving
thanks to God and the Father by him." In Colossians 3
notice the emphasis on the peace of Christ, the word of
Christ and the name of Christ. The exact statements are
"Let the peace of God rule in your hearts" (v. 15); "let the
word of Christ dwell in you richly" (v. 16); "do all in the name
of the Lord Jesus" (v. 17).

John 14:27 tells of the peace of Christ: "Peace I leave with
you, my peace I give unto you: not as the world giveth, give I
unto you. Let not your heart be troubled, neither let it be
afraid." John 16:33 tells of this same peace: "These things I
have spoken unto you, that in me ye might have peace. In the
world ye shall have tribulation: but be of good cheer; I have
overcome the world."

The Word of Christ is emphasized in John 15:7: "If ye
abide in me, and my words abide in you, ye shall ask what ye
will, and it shall be done unto you." Hebrews 4:12 emphasizes this same word: "For the word of God is quick [living],
and powerful, and sharper than any twoedged sword, pierc-
ing even to the dividing asunder of soul and spirit, and of the
joints and marrow, and is a discerner of the thoughts and
intents of the heart."

The name of Christ is emphasized in Philippians 2:9-11:
"Wherefore God also hath highly exalted him, and given
him a name which is above every name: that at the name of
Jesus every knee should bow, of things in heaven, and

things in earth, and things under the earth; and that every tongue should confess that Jesus Christ is Lord, to the glory of God the Father." Also Acts 4:12 tells of this name: "Neither is there salvation in any other: for there is none other name under heaven given among men, whereby we must be saved."

The peace of Christ, the Word of Christ and the name of Christ emphasize the all-sufficiency of Christ. And we are "complete in him" (Col. 2:10).

"The name of the Lord Jesus" (3:17) refers to His authority. When a document is signed, the authority of the person is associated with the document. In our society, we know the importance of a person's name on a check. This grants authority for money to be taken from that person's bank account and to be given to another.

As far as Christ is concerned, the authority relates to prayer, to resisting the Enemy and to checking our behavior.

That Christ's name means authority in prayer is evident from John 14:13,14: "And whatsoever ye shall ask in my name, that will I do, that the Father may be glorified in the Son. If ye shall ask any thing in my name, I will do it." In this regard notice also 15:16: "Ye have not chosen me, but I have chosen you, and ordained you, that ye should go and bring forth fruit, and that your fruit should remain: that whatsoever ye shall ask of the Father in my name, he may give it you."

The authority of Christ's name in prayer is also seen from John 16:23,24: "And in that day ye shall ask me nothing. Verily, verily, I say unto you, Whatsoever ye shall ask the Father in my name, he will give it you. Hitherto have ye asked nothing in my name: ask, and ye shall receive, that your joy may be full." All of the above verses reveal what it is to pray with authority.

That Christ's name means authority in resisting the Enemy is seen from I Peter 5:8,9: "Be sober, be vigilant; because your adversary the devil, as a roaring lion, walketh about, seeking whom he may devour: whom resist stedfast in the faith, knowing that the same afflictions are accomplished in your brethren that are in the world." Notice the statement in verse 9: "Whom resist stedfast in the faith." One might ask, What faith? Of course, it is referring to having confidence in Christ, but the answer could be "faith in the name of the Lord Jesus Christ."

The means of resisting the Enemy is also seen from James 4:7: "Submit yourselves therefore to God. Resist the devil, and he will flee from you." But when we do this, our submission is to all the authority of God, which resides in the name of the Lord Jesus Christ. In the seven-year Tribulation that is yet to come on the world, the Book of the Revelation tells us how Satan will be overcome by believers during that time. Revelation 12:10,11 says, "For the accuser of our brethren is cast down, which accused them before our God day and night. And they overcame him by the blood of the Lamb, and by the word of their testimony; and they loved not their lives unto the death."

That the name of the Lord Jesus Christ serves as a check on our behavior is seen from Paul's exhortation: "Do all in the name of the Lord Jesus" (Col. 3:17). In other words, we are to do everything we do in His name. If we cannot, it is wrong for us to do that specific thing. And notice the kinds of things Paul was referring to: "Whatsoever ye do in word or deed" (v. 17). If whatever we are doing or saying cannot be done to the glory of Christ's name, we are not to be doing it or saying it.

In this same regard, notice I Corinthians 10:31: "Whether therefore ye eat, or drink, or whatsoever ye do, do all to the glory of God." Especially notice the word "all" in this verse. Ephesians 5:20 also leaves out nothing: "Giving thanks always for all things unto God and the Father in the name of our Lord Jesus Christ." Notice that everything is also included in Philippians 4:6,7: "Be careful for nothing; but in every thing by prayer and supplication with thanksgiving let your requests be made known unto God. And the peace of God, which passeth all understanding, shall keep your hearts and minds through Christ Jesus."

Although bearing the name of the Lord Jesus Christ is a great privilege, it is also a great responsibility. Have you noticed both the attention and respect (though sometimes only outward) that people give you when they realize you are a Christian? I have noticed this especially on the golf course. Sometimes when it is crowded, two of us are put with another twosome. In such a situation it is customary to hear a lot of cursing as the players get frustrated with their games. But what a change comes over them when they learn that one in their group is a Christian! Of course, the respect is often only outward, but still it shows that the name of Christ makes a difference to them.

Also consider what some people expect when they know we are Christians. They will especially observe how we live and what we say. The world has a standard by which it judges us. And if you fall short of that standard, you will hear something such as "Well! And he says he's a Christian!"

So it is a great responsibility to bear the name of Christ. We who know Him as Saviour are watched. With the eyes of others on us, we must live and talk in a way that causes them to want to know our Lord.

In this regard, Peter gave wives instructions on how to win their unsaved husbands who were watching their behavior. Peter said, "Wives, in the same way be submissive to your husbands so that, if any of them do not believe the word, they may be won over without talk by the behavior of their wives, when they see the purity and reverence of your lives. Your beauty should not come from outward adornment, such as braided hair and the wearing of gold jewelry and fine clothes. Instead, it should be that of your inner self, the unfading beauty of a gentle and quiet spirit, which is of great worth in God's sight" (I Pet. 3:1-4, NIV).

One cannot help but be impressed by the centrality of Christ in everything that pertains to our spiritual life. The peace of Christ is to be the ruling factor, or umpire, in our lives. The Word of Christ is to dwell in us richly as the basis of spiritual growth and inward transformation. And the name of Christ serves as our true identification and authority. Truly, "Christ is all, and in all" (Col. 3:11).

By the indwelling Holy Spirit, we have in Christ all our resources for holy living. The Lord Jesus Christ has "given unto us all things that pertain unto life and godliness" (II Pet. 1:3). What a wonderful God we have! No wonder Paul said, "Whatsoever ye do in word or deed, do all in the name of the Lord Jesus, giving thanks to God and the Father by him" (Col. 3:17).

Chapter 9

The Christian Home

Colossians 1 and 2 emphasize doctrine, and 3 and 4 emphasize practice. And when talking about practicing the Christian faith, Paul saw the home as the central place where the graces of Christ were to be evident. Some people can put on a front and seem to live a victorious Christian life among those who do not know them well, but what are they like in the home?

The portion of Colossians that especially treats the aspect of home life is 3:18—4:1, but this is not the only passage in Scripture that addresses the Christian home. Ephesians 5:21—6:9 and I Peter 3:1-7 are passages which should also be studied.

The focus of Colossians 3:18—4:1 is not just any home but a Christian home. Those who do not know Jesus Christ as personal Saviour do not have the capacity, or enablement, to live out the qualities mentioned by Paul. Christ is the center of the Christian home because He is the center in the lives of the individuals in the home.

The home was the first institution founded by God (see Gen. 2:18-25; Matt. 19:3-6). Yet the Scriptures indicate that in the end times there will be a breakdown of the home (see II Tim. 3:1-5). This will be true not only in North America but also around the world. And we see this breakdown occurring at the present time. Many are living together without being married—not only younger people but older ones too. Many babies are being killed by means of abortion, and many others are born out of wedlock. These are the direct results of a society in which the people love their pleasures and themselves more than they love God. Even this is a fulfillment of what Paul said would be the condition in the end times: "For men shall be lovers of their own selves" (II Tim. 3:2). The statement, "Without natural affection" (v. 3), especially emphasizes that they will be without family love. Keeping in mind that the home is in for some exceedingly rough days during the end times, let us now see what Paul said about the home in Colossians 3.

Responsibilities of Husbands and Wives

First, Paul addressed husbands and wives. He commanded, "Wives, submit yourselves unto you own husbands, as it is fit in the Lord. Husbands, love your wives, and be not bitter against them" (Col. 3:18,19).

Paul told the wives they should submit. The Greek word translated "submit" is a military term meaning "to arrange under" or "to rank under." This in no way means that the wife is inferior to her husband; rather, it means that for the home to function properly the wife ranks under her husband, who is the one responsible to God. Even this indicates that God is a God of order. He has not left each home to decide which person will be responsible to Him for what happens in the home—He has made the husband directly responsible. It is always God's concern that "all things be done decently and in order" (I Cor. 14:40), and He has specified what the order should be for the home. The responsibility for the spiritual and physical well-being of the home rests upon the husband, and the wife ranks under him in this regard.

It is important to note that headship does not mean dictatorship. Ephesians 5:21 indicates that there is to be a submission of both to the lordship of Christ and to each other: "Submitting yourselves one to another in the fear of God." The husband and wife are to be loyal to each other; in fact, at least one commentator gives evidence that the word "submit" can be translated "loyal." In the Scripture passages emphasizing the Christian home, it is apparent that the husband and wife are viewed as being one in Christ. And all of the submission is to be "in the Lord." But as far as function in the home is concerned, God holds one more responsible than the other, and in this regard the wife ranks under the husband. This rank is also seen in I Corinthians 11:3: "But I would have you know, that the head of every man is Christ; and the head of the woman is the man; and the head of Christ is God." Even though the woman ranks under the man, she is not inferior to him any more than Christ is inferior to God, although in this verse as far as function is concerned Christ ranks under the Father.

Having commanded the wives to submit "as it is fit in the Lord" (Col. 3:18), Paul commanded, "Husbands, love your wives, and be not bitter against them" (v. 19). The love mentioned in this verse is *agape,* which is self-giving and always seeks the other person's highest good. Ephesians 5:25 gives a comparison to show how much husbands are to love their wives: "Love your wives, even as Christ also loved the church, and gave himself for it." This is the kind of love the husband is to have for his wife, and this is certainly not possible unless he is a Christian. The unbelieving husband may genuinely love his wife and show her respect, but the husband who knows Christ as Saviour has a greater capacity to love, for he realizes how much the Lord Jesus Christ loves him.

The phrase, "be not bitter against them" (Col. 3:19), can be compared with Ephesians 5:28,29: "So ought men to love their wives as their own bodies. He that loveth his wife loveth himself. For no man ever yet hated his own flesh; but nourisheth and cherisheth it, even as the Lord the church." Thus, we see that the husband's love for his wife is a self-giving love. As someone has said, "Love is not a mere feeling but a fact, not merely emotion but devotion, not mere attitude but action, not mere sentiment but sacrifice."

The word used for love in these passages on the home reveals that it is much more than an emotional response; it is a determination of the will. If it were only emotional, the husband would love his wife only when she responded favorably. But the husband is commanded to seek his wife's highest good in all things by an act of the will, whether she responds favorably or not.

Husbands are commanded to love their wives "and be not bitter against them" (Col. 3:19). Husbands will be helped in this if they remember that they are to love their wives "even as Christ also loved the church, and gave himself for it" (Eph. 5:25). Although there was nothing deserving in us, Christ willingly and lovingly gave Himself for our sins. "While we were yet sinners, Christ died for us" (Rom. 5:8). Certainly, Jesus Christ would have been totally justified if

He had become bitter toward us and done nothing for our salvation. But He gave Himself for our sins. And this is the same loving attitude that husbands are to have for their wives. The same basic word for love used in the key passages on marriage is also used in I Corinthians 13. Notice the qualities of love mentioned in verses 4 and 5: "Love is patient, love is kind. It does not envy, it does not boast, it is not proud. It is not rude, it is not self-seeking, it is not easily angered, it keeps no record of wrongs" (NIV). When a wife has a husband who loves her with these kinds of qualities, she will have little trouble in submitting, or being loyal, to him. She will realize that he plans and works in her behalf and for her good.

Responsibilities of Children

In treating the subject of the Christian home, Paul next emphasized the responsibility of children. Paul commanded, "Children, obey your parents in all things: for this is well pleasing unto the Lord" (Col. 3:20). Children need to realize that to obey is pleasing to the Lord. Children are to obey in all things, not just in those things which please them.

Children who know Jesus Christ as Saviour must remember that both they and their parents are members of the same Body with the same Head (Christ). Thus, Christian family members are fellow members of the Body of Christ. If the parents fulfill their proper role under Christ's authority; that is, the wife submitting to the husband and the husband loving the wife as he should (vv. 18,19), the children have a good example to follow. However, if the parents are not submitting to the proper authority (the wife to the husband and the husband to Christ), they will not be able to exercise authority over others, including their children.

The responsibility of the parents, especially of the father, is emphasized in verse 21: "Fathers, provoke not your children to anger, lest they be discouraged." Both parents should be careful in this regard; so this command could be applied to both father and mother. However, the word Paul used means specifically "fathers," and perhaps that is because Paul realized that fathers—more than mothers—tend to provoke their children.

A godly couple will want to work together to produce a spiritual climate in the home so it is as easy as possible for the children to obey quickly and pleasantly. The responsibility of both parents in caring for the children is seen from what Moses' parents did for him: "By faith Moses, when he was born, was hid three months of his parents" (Heb. 11:23). The historical account given in Exodus 2 emphasizes what his mother did, but Hebrews 11:23 reveals that both parents took responsibility.

Parents, do you make it easy for your children to obey? Do you provide a climate in the home that encourages them or irritates them?

All of us who have grown children look back and realize that we did things that were not always best, even though we did what we thought was best at the time. No parent is perfect, and you should not apologize because you are not perfect. However, from the experience Mrs. Epp and I have had, as well as from observing others, I present the following questions for you to consider. Do you listen to your children? Do you have a reason when you say no? (Not that you always have to explain the reason, but do you have one?) Are you honest with your children? (If you are not, it is highly inconsistent of you to discipline them for not being honest with you and others.) Do you consider your children a bother or a blessing? (Admittedly, the responsibility of children is at times inconvenient, but do you recognize the blessing of having children and being able to mold their lives for the glory of Christ?) Do you spend time with your children? (Later, when they are grown and away from home, it will be the time you spent with them that will mean the most, not the things you gave them.)

Father, how well can you answer these questions? If you are not doing what you know you should be doing, are you taking steps in the right direction as far as your relationship with your children is concerned?

The problems of our children may seem small to us, but they are big to them. It is important for parents to maintain order and harmony in the home through proper discipline, but be careful of being too severe. Perhaps the most difficult thing to achieve in discipline is balance. Some parents exercise no discipline, which produces its own set of serious problems. On the other hand, some parents discipline too severely, thereby losing the respect of their children and driving them from the home, the church and God.

Christian young people do not have it easy today. This is a very complex age in which to face the various circumstances of life and take a stand for Christ. Above all, they need parents who are loving and concerned about their best interests.

It is important for the parents to be in agreement on the discipline, or child training, that will be exercised. Nothing is accomplished if the children are allowed to pit father against mother or mother against father. Parents should stand unified before their children, and personal differences about discipline should be worked out behind the scenes between the parents, or else more confusion and frustration will result between the children and the parents.

Responsibilities of Servants and Masters

In this same portion of Colossians, Paul also gave instructions to servants and masters (3:22—4:1). The relationship between servants and masters can be compared to that of employees and employers today. Although not directly related to home life as we normally think of it, the relationship of employer and employee grows out of the home and certainly affects the home.

Paul commanded, "Servants, obey in all things your masters according to the flesh; not with eyeservice, as menpleasers; but in singleness of heart, fearing God: and whatsoever you do, do it heartily, as to the Lord, and not unto men; knowing that of the Lord ye shall receive the reward of the inheritance: for ye serve the Lord Christ. But he that doeth wrong shall receive for the wrong which he hath done: and there is no respect of persons" (vv. 22-25).

Admonition to Servants

These verses contain a sevenfold admonition to servants. First, "Obey in all things" (v. 22). From the context it is evident that this obedience is to be toward both one's earthly master and one's heavenly Master.

Second, this obedience is to be "not with eyeservice"

(v. 22). The Christian servant should be faithful in working all of the time, not just when his master is watching him. Even when his earthly master does not see him, his heavenly Master does.

Third, servants who know Christ as Saviour should not serve "as menpleasers" (v. 22). The believer is not a man pleaser but a Christ pleaser. As a result, his work will be of high quality, and most masters will be pleased with it.

Fourth, the believing servant is to serve "in singleness of heart, fearing God" (v. 22). "Singleness of heart" implies a heart that is fixed on one goal—that of honoring Jesus Christ in everything. Another version translates verse 22: "Servants, obey in everything those who are your earthly masters, not only when their eyes are on you, as pleasers of men, but in simplicity of purpose (with all your heart) because of your reverence for the Lord and as a sincere expression of your devotion to Him" (Amplified).

Thus, whatever Christian servants do, they are to "do it heartily" (v. 23). The Christian should never be one who works halfheartedly; rather, he should work with all his heart. He should work with enthusiasm and do the best job possible because he realizes he is ultimately seeking to please the Lord. One of the best ways a Christian can be a testimony when working with unbelievers is to take a sincere interest in his work and do the best job possible. Unbelievers will recognize there is something different about that kind of person. Halfhearted work is a poor testimony, and a believer who works this way should not expect to have an effective witness among his fellow workers.

Sixth, whatever work the believer does, he is to do it "as to the Lord, and not unto men" (v. 23). When you are motivated to please the Lord in what you do, you will not do halfhearted work. The Christian employee who truly seeks to please the Lord will be a good testimony to his boss and to fellow employees. No matter how tedious the job, it becomes more important when one realizes that he is doing it to please God, not just men.

Seventh, a Christian employee should do his work with all his heart because he realizes his work will someday be judged by the Lord. He will receive a reward for that which he has done well. "Knowing that of the Lord ye shall receive the reward of the inheritance: for ye serve the Lord Christ" (v. 24).

However, there is also the negative aspect of this judgment: "But he that doeth wrong shall receive for the wrong which he hath done: and there is no respect of persons" (v. 25).

Each one who knows Jesus Christ as Saviour will someday stand before the Judgment Seat of Christ to be rewarded for the things done in this life. Writing by inspiration of the Holy Spirit, Paul said concerning this judgment, "Wherefore we labour, that, whether present or absent, we may be accepted of him. For we must all appear before the judgment seat of Christ; that every one may receive the things done in his body, according to that he hath done, whether it be good or bad" (II Cor. 5:9,10).

Both the good and bad we do will be judged. This not only involves so-called Christian work but all work of the believer—in the office, shop, farm, factory. And each Christian will be evaluated, for "there is no respect of persons" (Col. 3:25). From top leadership to the lowliest worker, all will be judged, "for ye serve the Lord Christ" (v. 24).

Admonition to Masters

In addition to giving specific commands to Christian employees, Paul also gave clear commands to Christian employers: "Masters, give unto your servants that which is just and equal; knowing that ye also have a Master in heaven" (Col. 4:1). The Christian employer is commanded to pay his employees what is justly due them and also to treat them "equal," or with fairness.

The actual situation being addressed by Paul was a master-slave relationship, but even then we see that the masters were to treat their slaves with consideration for the value of the person. Onesimus was a slave of Philemon, and as Paul wrote to Philemon in behalf of Onesimus, he said, "I appeal to you for my son Onesimus, who became my son while I was in chains. Formerly he was useless to you, but now he has become useful both to you and to me. I am sending him—who is my very heart—back to you" (Philem. 1:10-12, NIV). Concerning the value of Onesimus, Paul told Philemon: "No longer as a slave, but better than a slave, as a dear brother. He is very dear to me but even dearer to you, both as a man and as a brother in the Lord" (v. 16, NIV). Notice that Onesimus was to be treated as a person and as a brother, even though he was a slave.

Paul warned employers to treat their employees well, "knowing that ye also have a Master in heaven" (Col. 4:1). If the employer puts Christ first (gives Him preeminence) in his life and leadership, he will treat his employee right and also face his own Master in heaven with a clear conscience and a clean heart.

Christian employer, are you fair with your employees? Do you treat them as you would like to be treated? Are you honest and above board with your employees? (You may not need to give them all the details, but are you open and honest with them, or do you seek to manipulate them?) Do you treat your employees as persons with real value, and do you treat each believer as your brother in Christ?

Notice throughout this entire passage in Colossians how the home and work are to give Christ preeminence. The passage reveals that "Christ is all, and in all" (3:11). Paul instructed those in the home and at work that everything was to be done for the Lord. Notice the following six references:

"Wives, submit . . . in the Lord" (v. 18).

"Children, obey . . . unto the Lord" (v. 20).

"Servants, obey . . . fearing God" (v. 22).

"[Servants] . . . do it . . . as to the Lord" (v. 23).

"[Servants] ye serve the Lord Christ" (v. 24).

"Masters . . . ye also have a Master in heaven" (4:1).

The above emphasis reveals that Christ must be the center of all the believer's activity. The Christian who lives a shallow or disobedient life does not really believe in the all-sufficiency of Christ. Such a believer is a discredit to his earthly master and is really denying his heavenly Master.

Chapter 10

Practical Advice and Further Instructions

Having given commands concerning the home and work to believers, Paul stated, "Continue in prayer, and watch in the same with thanksgiving; withal praying also for us, that God would open unto us a door of utterance, to speak the mystery of Christ, for which I am also in bonds: that I may make it manifest, as I ought to speak. Walk in wisdom toward them that are without, redeeming the time. Let your speech be alway with grace, seasoned with salt, that ye may know how ye ought to answer every man" (Col. 4:2-6).

The content of these verses serves as an application of what is stated in Philippians 2:12,13: "Work out your own salvation with fear and trembling. For it is God which work-eth in you both to will and to do of his good pleasure." The Holy Spirit has come to take up residence in the believer; so it is important that he work out, or express, the salvation that is within him.

Colossians 4:2-6 serves as a further application of making Christ preeminent in one's personal experience. In this passage, Paul spoke of prayer that is to be practiced (vv. 2-4), wise conduct toward the unsaved (v. 5), proper use of time (v. 5) and sound and gracious speech (v. 6).

Practice of Prayer

First, notice the practice of prayer (Col. 4:2-4).

Faithful in Prayer

Paul instructed the believers in Colossae to "continue in prayer" (Col. 4:2). That is, he desired that believers always maintain the habit of prayer. The Greek word translated "continue in" means "be busily engaged in" or "give constant attention to." This does not mean that a person walks

163

around with eyes half closed and hands folded while saying one long prayer. The meaning is that an individual is to be in fellowship with God, but he will not necessarily always be talking to God in prayer. In this regard, I Thessalonians 5:17 says, "Pray without ceasing." The word translated "without ceasing" was used in Bible times of a person with an incessant cough. It was not one long, drawn-out cough but was coughing at frequent intervals. So, too, we will pray at frequent intervals. We are always to maintain the habit of prayer and to be in constant readiness for prayer. Our praying should be faithful and steadfast.

The early church was faithful in prayer. In fact, when the 120 met in the upper room, it was for the purpose of prayer. Acts 1:14 says, "These all continued with one accord in prayer and supplication." When the Day of Pentecost arrived, they were still continuing "all with one accord in one place" (2:1).

Praying should be as natural for the believer as breathing. We don't even have to think about breathing; we do it automatically. So, too, throughout the day we should be constantly ready to talk to God about the various details of life. I once had missionary friends with me as I was driving around the block looking for a parking place. Quietly, without paying any attention to them, I said, "Lord, I need a parking place." Just then someone began backing out ahead of us. The missionary looked at me and said, "Do you talk to God about everything?" "I sure do," I said. "It's just a habit." I do not know that I do it as much as I should, but I constantly talk to God like this about various details of life.

Watchful in Prayer

Paul urged the believers not only to "continue in prayer" (Col. 4:2) but also to "watch in the same with thanksgiving" (v. 2). We are to be alert in our praying. The Greek word translated "watch" means "to give strict attention to." We should mean business in our prayer life and be careful that other things do not keep us from regular times of prayer.

We should also watch lest we just *say* prayers. Especially in public praying, long prayers may produce a restlessness and inattentiveness among those who listen.

We must always guard against our prayers becoming a

form, or ritual. Mrs. Epp and I have our private devotions, but we also enjoy reading the Word together and praying together at the breakfast table. But even that could become just a habit.

As W. H. Griffith Thomas has said, "We are not to watch ourselves, which would be depressing; we are not to watch Satan, which would be distracting; we are not to watch our sins, which would be disheartening, but we are to keep our gaze fixed on Christ" (*Christ Pre-eminent,* pp. 108,109). Hebrews 12:2 reveals where we are to keep our attention fixed: "Looking unto Jesus the author and finisher of our faith."

Thankful in Prayer

That prayer is to be made "with thanksgiving" (Col. 4:2) is also emphasized by Philippians 4:6: "Be careful for nothing; but in every thing by prayer and supplication with thanksgiving let your requests be made known unto God." Thanksgiving with prayer is the proof of faith. True faith does not have to see the answer before it thanks God. When we pray, we can say, "Lord, I thank You that You are going to answer this prayer in the way that You believe will be best for me, and I thank You for it now." This is accepting the answer by faith.

Purposeful in Prayer

To the believers in Colossae, Paul stated further, "Withal praying also for us" (Col. 4:3). "Withal" refers to the Colossians' remembering Paul and his associates when they prayed for others. This phrase could be translated "while praying also for us."

Paul was not ashamed to ask his friends to pray for him. He was a leader and an apostle, but he felt deeply in need of the prayer support of fellow believers. I am afraid that sometimes people think that Christian leaders are infallible—or at least that they do not need prayer. Although God has given me the privilege of being in the forefront of the Back to the Bible ministry, I and the ministry are greatly in need of your prayers. I am convinced that prayer is the secret of God's work. Many of the people praying for Paul probably did not know where he was or what he was doing at the time they were praying. But Paul wanted them to be faithful in praying for him anyhow.

Prayer should always be purposeful and as specific as possible. We need to learn all we can about the individuals for whom we pray, as well as the circumstances surrounding them. As a result, we will be able to pray specifically for them, even though we do not know on a given day what they may be doing. The more we know about the needs of the individual and the circumstances he faces, the easier it will be to keep from praying a vague prayer such as, "God, bless the missionary."

Because of our commitment to the importance of prayer, Back to the Bible sends requests to its Prayer Partners so they can more intelligently pray for the ministry. We also devised a Scripture Text Calendar that lists prayer requests for each day. We are convinced of the power of prayer, and I must admit that I am thrilled when I notice my name on a particular day and realize that all over the world believers are remembering me in prayer on that day.

Someone once asked Spurgeon what the secret of his success was. His answer was simple: "My people pray for me." On another occasion he showed a visitor the lower auditorium of his church. "Here," he said, "is our power house. While I am preaching upstairs, hundreds of people are down here praying."

Notice the two specific prayer requests which Paul gave the believers in Colossae: "That God would open unto us a door of utterance, to speak the mystery of Christ, for which I am also in bonds" (v. 3) and "that I may make it manifest, as I ought to speak" (v. 4).

Paul did not ask for prison doors to be opened but that the doors of his ministry might be opened. Paul spoke of an open door of ministry in I Corinthians 16:9: "For a great door and effectual is opened unto me, and there are many adversaries." Acts 14:27 speaks of the opportunities that Paul and Barnabas had to minister the Gospel: "And when they were come, and had gathered the church together, they rehearsed all that God had done with them, and how he had opened the door of faith unto the Gentiles."

Acts 16 records how Paul and Silas were beaten and cast into prison. The miraculous working of God eventually released them. Read especially verses 23-26, and notice that there is no indication that Paul and Silas were praying to be released from prison. In fact, there is no evidence in Paul's prison epistles that he ever prayed for personal release. But he did pray for strength to face the circumstances in which he found himself. But as Paul was praying for opportunities to witness, God often did other dramatic things, such as bringing about Paul's release in Philippi.

As Paul wrote his letter to the believers in Colossae, he was a prisoner in Rome. Yet he did not ask them to pray for his release but that "God would open unto us a door of utterance, to speak the mystery of Christ" (Col. 4:3). Paul wanted an open door to talk to others about Jesus Christ.

Not only was Paul being kept in prison, but most likely he was chained to a guard. You can imagine how Paul must have talked to that guard in an endeavor to bring him to a saving knowledge of the Lord Jesus Christ. Various soldiers would take turns guarding Paul, which gave him more opportunities to talk about Christ.

Because of Paul's special circumstances, he had the opportunity to witness in places that otherwise would have been inaccessible to him. As a prisoner, he was able to declare Jesus Christ in the court of Rome, which he would have been unable to do had he been free. Various references in the Scriptures indicate that Paul had converts from these contacts. For instance, he told the believers in Philippi: "All the saints salute you, chiefly they that are of Caesar's household" (Phil. 4:22).

In our day, one sometimes hears about "closed doors" as far as certain mission fields of the world are concerned. But in a very real sense, there is no such thing as a closed door. Radio, in particular, is able to jump all barriers and to reach people right where they live. We once received a letter from a missionary, telling us he had heard our broadcast (being aired from Ceylon, now called Sri Lanka) while visiting in Russia. Think of that! The message had crossed India as well as other smaller countries and had reached into Russia. Not only did those in Russia have the opportunity to hear, but also the countries in between had the opportunity to receive the signal and hear the Gospel.

Christian radio needs the faithful prayer support of those

who love Christ and want the Gospel message to be effective as it reaches the hearts of a lost world. Of course, many need to give to support Christian radio so the Gospel can be sent out, but it is desperately important that believers pray so the message will be effective in the hearts of those who hear. Never say, "The least I can do is pray." That is the greatest thing you can do. Consider that not only important but a vital part of reaching a lost world with the Gospel.

Paul wanted the Gospel to be heard, but he also wanted it to be expressed with the most effectiveness possible: "That I may make it manifest, as I ought to speak" (Col. 4:4). What a reminder this is for all of us. We do not need to wait for a different set of circumstances to be more effective; we need prayer and wisdom so that we can be more effective right where we are.

Conduct Toward the Unsaved

Paul commanded the Colossians, "Walk in wisdom toward them that are without" (Col. 4:5). The word translated "walk" emphasizes the daily conduct of the individual. Elsewhere, the Bible commands, "That ye may walk honestly toward them that are without" (I Thess. 4:12). Are you honest in your business dealings with others? If you have promised to pay bills, do you pay them promptly?

"Them that are without" is a reference to those who are outside the group of believers—unbelievers. One of the best ways the believer can be a witness to unbelievers—and earn the right to talk to them about their salvation—is by being upright and honest in all of his business dealings. Once it is known that a person is a Christian, others will watch him or her carefully to see how he or she lives. This is true whether the believer is an older person or a younger person.

I remember with delight when one of our daughters was a young girl in school. She did her best to witness as she could. A report got back to us later through another person that apparently even the teacher had been deeply touched by our daughter's witnessing and had indicated that if she became a Christian, she wanted to be like our daughter. This shows that the world watches us closely.

Another example of this was included among the many appreciated cards and letters which I received for my 75th birthday in January, 1982. A former Nebraska governor, who had been Back to the Bible's attorney for several years, wrote a commendation about the way Back to the Bible handles its finances and indicated it was something to be emulated. It was especially an encouraging remark from this person who knew the organization so well, and it also caused me to realize again that others watch us as believers in Christ to see how we live and handle our business.

Christians must always be concerned about how they can present the message in a way that will appeal to others rather than turn them off. First Peter 3:1,2 tells wives how to reach their unsaved husbands: "Wives, in the same way be submissive to your husbands so that, if any of them do not believe the word, they may be won over without talk by the behavior of their wives, when they see the purity and reverence of your lives" (NIV). There are principles in these verses that apply to all witnessing.

A good testimony to unbelievers is so important that it is considered one of the qualifications for church leadership. "Moreover he must have a good report of them which are without" (I Tim. 3:7). If a Christian does not have a good testimony in the world, he is not qualified to be a leader of a local church. Imagine how the business community would look on a church if it had a leader whom they knew had not been honest and fair in his dealings with them. The world would not take such a church seriously, and the testimony of the church would be damaged. A good verse for believers to keep in mind is II Corinthians 8:21: "Providing for honest things, not only in the sight of the Lord, but also in th sight of men."

Use of Time

Paul also told the Colossian believers that they should be "redeeming the time" (Col. 4:5). Paul wanted the believers to buy up every opportunity—to make wise and sacred use of every opportunity for doing good.

Paul especially wanted the Colossians to seize every opportunity to do good to those without and thus to increase the effective outreach of the Gospel. We should never allow an opportunity to be lost. Once an opportunity is gone, it may never occur again.

We should not be so nervous about available opportunities that we are unable to take full advantage of them. We should simply develop the habit of using our time wisely and properly and be sensitive to those occasions when we can witness for Christ or demonstrate proper Christian living.

The thought of Colossians 4:5 is also expressed in Ephesians 5:16: "Redeeming the time, because the days are evil." Paul was a good example of one who used every opportunity—whether in prison or out of prison—to witness for Christ. Paul had the opportunity to witness before governors, rulers and guards as he was being tried in the courts of the Roman Empire. Read Acts 24 to see the opportunity Paul had to present the Gospel to Felix. There is no evidence that Felix became a Christian, but he clearly heard the Gospel from the lips of Paul. Paul probably would not have had the opportunity to witness to Felix had he not been a prisoner in Rome. We do not know whether Paul ever had the opportunity to talk to Caesar personally, but if he did, we can be sure he presented a clear Gospel message.

Paul stated in Ephesians 5:16 the reason for redeeming the time: "The days are evil." We do not know how long we will have to freely proclaim the Gospel. Even now, some countries of the world have passed laws that make it extremely difficult for believers to share their faith. We in North America are privileged at this time to be able to freely share our faith. Let us not take these times for granted.

Also, no one knows how long it will be until the Lord returns to catch away believers from the earth. This time may be very close at hand. We need to give out the Gospel while we can. Those to whom we are witnessing now may not live much longer even if Christ's coming is not until several years from now. So we need to be more conscious of taking advantage of opportunities *now*.

Verses that encouraged us so much when we first started the Back to the Bible ministry are just as true today. I refer to Revelation 3:7,8: "And to the angel of the church in Philadelphia write; These things saith he that is holy, he that is true, he that hath the key of David, he that openeth, and no man shutteth; and shutteth, and no man openeth; I know thy works: behold, I have set before thee an open door, and no man can shut it: for thou hast a little strength, and hast kept my word, and hast not denied my name." God is able to open the doors, and it is important that we act now, for we do not know how much longer these opportunities will exist.

Graciousness in Speech

Paul also instructed the Colossians, "Let your speech be alway with grace, seasoned with salt, that ye may know how ye ought to answer every man" (Col. 4:6). It is important that we live a consistent Christian life, but living alone is not enough. We must also speak so others know of the need to trust Christ as their Saviour. No one can know specific facts about sin, Jesus Christ, salvation by grace through faith and eternal life just by viewing our consistent lives. At some point, the message must be presented. That's when a consistent life is needed to back up the message.

Romans 10:13-15 reveals the importance of declaring the Gospel as well as living it. Verse 13 says, "Whosoever shall call upon the name of the Lord shall be saved." But notice the following verses which reveal that specific information must be given: "How then shall they call on him in whom they have not believed? and how shall they believe in him of whom they have not heard? and how shall they hear without a preacher? and how shall they preach, except they be sent? as it is written, How beautiful are the feet of them that preach the gospel of peace, and bring glad tidings of good things!" (vv. 14,15).

Controlled by Grace

Paul wanted the Colossians not only to have the right thing to say but to use the right manner in saying it. *The Amplified Bible* translates Colossians 4:6: "Let your speech at all times be gracious (pleasant and winsome), seasoned [as it were] with salt, [so that you may never be at a loss] to know how you ought to answer any one [who puts a question to you]."

Our speech should be controlled by grace, which means that we must be filled, or controlled, by the Holy Spirit. Colossians 3:16 says, "Let the word of Christ dwell in you richly," and Ephesians 5:18 says, "Be filled with the Spirit." As the Word of God controls our lives, our speech will be controlled by grace; therefore, our words will be gracious. We will still speak the truth, but we will speak "the truth in love" (Eph. 4:15). When the Gospel is spoken in love, it makes such a difference in the way it is received.

Seasoned With Salt

Paul urged the Colossians to let their speech be "seasoned with salt" (Col. 4:6). Salt makes food more flavorful. Paul wanted believers to speak in such a way that others would be attracted to the Gospel.

Salt also serves as a preservative. Those who are older will remember when meat was salted to preserve it. Paul may have also had purity of speech in mind. He told the Ephesians, "Let no corrupt communication proceed out of your mouth, but that which is good to the use of edifying, that it may minister grace unto the hearers" (Eph. 4:29).

Let us not forget, however, that salt rubbed into wounds can hurt. Paul did not have this use in mind. He wanted believers to use comforting and encouraging speech which would also convey truth concerning the unbeliever's needs. We need to avoid thoughtless words of criticism which tear others down rather than edifying them. We also must avoid angry words. Then there is the matter of "shady" words, which do not honor the Lord. Each of us needs to carefully consider how our speech affects others—both positively and negatively. Paul's statement of Colossians 4:6, "that ye may know how ye ought to answer every man," is a reminder of I Peter 3:15: "But sanctify the Lord God in your hearts: and be ready always to give an answer to every man that asketh you a reason of the hope that is in you with meekness and fear."

This again points back to the importance of having the Word in our minds, hearts and souls. Some believers think that if they just rely on the Holy Spirit, they will be given answers to questions, even though they did not know the information previously. This is an unrealistic view of the ministry of the Holy Spirit. As we are constantly studying the Word of God, thinking about what it says and applying it to our lives, we can count on the Holy Spirit to bring facts to our minds when we need to answer someone. But if we have never studied the Word for ourselves, there is nothing for the Holy Spirit to bring to our attention. So it is important to "let the word of Christ dwell in you richly" (Col. 3:16). The Holy Spirit can only use the Word you have hidden in your heart through personal devotional and study time. This will enable you to be ready with an answer for those who ask about your faith.

Paul was always ready to answer anyone who questioned what he believed. Notice three statements he made in his Epistle to the Romans: "I am debtor" (1:14), "I am not ashamed" (v. 16) and "I am ready to preach" (v. 15). Can we say these things? Is our walk in harmony with what we say? Someone has well said, "When character, conduct and conversation are all working together, it makes for a powerful witness." What kind of witness are you?

Friends of Paul

As Paul concluded his letter to the Colossians, he was careful to mention several dedicated friends and co-laborers (Col. 4:7-18). I think I can understand what was going through his mind. In the many years of ministry at Back to the Bible, I have deeply appreciated those who have served with me, and they have not gotten the honor they have deserved. Such co-workers are "labourers together with God" (I Cor. 3:9).

Some of the dedicated friends and co-workers Paul specifically mentioned in his letter to the Colossians were Timothy, Tychicus, Onesimus, Epaphras, Luke and Demas.

Timothy

Timothy is not mentioned at the end of the letter as are the others, but he was specifically singled out at the beginning of the letter: "Paul, an apostle of Jesus Christ by the will of God, and Timotheus our brother" (Col. 1:1). How highly Paul thought of Timothy is seen from Philippians 2:19-22: "But I trust in the Lord Jesus to send Timotheus shortly unto you, that I also may be of good comfort, when I know your state. For I have no man likeminded, who will naturally care for your state. For all seek their own, not the things which are Jesus Christ's. But ye know the proof of him, that, as a son with the father, he hath served with me in the gospel."

Paul knew there were few people like Timothy who selflessly served the cause of Christ rather than their own interests. I, too, wish to praise God for the people He has sent to work on the Back to the Bible staff. They have been more concerned about the glory of Christ than about their own promotion in life, and God has honored them for it.

Tychicus

The other men Paul singled out for special recognition are mentioned at the close of his letter. Paul called attention to Tychicus: "All my state shall Tychicus declare unto you, who is a beloved brother, and a faithful minister and fellow-servant in the Lord. Whom I have sent unto you for the same purpose, that he might know your estate, and comfort your hearts" (Col. 4:7,8).

Notice the three ways Paul described Tychicus. First, he was "a beloved brother" (v. 7). This indicates the interest and concern the two had for each other. Paul loved Tychicus as a brother in Christ.

Second, Paul referred to Tychicus as "a faithful minister [servant]" (v. 7). Paul said nothing about his brilliance or outstanding ability but simply stated that he was faithful. Recognition for faithfulness is possibly the greatest compliment one can receive. The Bible says, "It is required in stewards, that a man be found faithful" (I Cor. 4:2). One of the most disappointing traits found among Christians today is that so many cannot be counted on. Many are well trained and bright, but they are not faithful. Tychicus was dependable.

Matthew 25:21 shows that the Lord is looking for faithfulness: "His lord said unto him, Well done, thou good and faithful servant: thou hast been faithful over a few things, I will make thee ruler over many things: enter thou into the joy of thy lord." Read the Book of Daniel, and notice the favor he gained, even among unbelievers, because others realized he was dependable. He could be counted on when very few others could be. In fact, it was extremely difficult for his jealous enemies to trap him because they could find nothing to accuse him of. Daniel 6:4 says, "Then the presidents and princes sought to find occasion against Daniel concerning the kingdom; but they could find none occasion nor fault; forasmuch as he was faithful, neither was there any error or fault found in him." When the Lord comes, will He find us faithful?

Paul also mentioned concerning Tychicus that he was a "fellowservant in the Lord" (Col. 4:7). Paul had labored with him. Even though Paul was an apostle, he did not feel superior to Tychicus; he considered him a "fellowservant."

Onesimus

Paul next singled out Onesimus for special attention: "With Onesimus, a faithful and beloved brother, who is one of you" (Col. 4:9). Notice that he, too, was considered faithful. He had been a runaway slave, according to the Book of Philemon. Perhaps he was not the best of servants when he was with Philemon, and he may have even stolen some things as he was running away. But Paul had won him to the Lord, and now Onesimus was returning to Philemon to make things right. Think about it! A runaway slave had become "a faithful and beloved brother" to the Apostle Paul.

Epaphras

Another especially singled out by Paul was Epaphras: "Epaphras, who is one of you, a servant of Christ, saluteth you, always labouring fervently for you in prayers, that ye may stand perfect and complete in all the will of God. For I bear him record, that he hath a great zeal for you, and them that are in Laodicea, and them in Hierapolis" (Col. 4:12,13).

Epaphras was possibly the teacher and founder of the church in Colossae. In particular, he had brought information to Paul concerning the Colossians: "As ye also learned of Epaphras our dear fellowservant, who is for you a faithful minister of Christ; who also declared unto us your love in the Spirit" (1:7,8).

Epaphras was not returning to Colossae at this time, for apparently he was a prisoner along with Paul. But even though he was a prisoner, he continued to pray fervently for the Colossians. Commenting on verse 12, *The Scofield Reference Bible* states: "A touching illustration of priestly service (see 1 Pet. 2.9, *note*) as distinguished from ministry of gift. Shut up in prison, no longer able to preach, Epaphras was still, equally with all believers, a priest. No prison could keep him from the throne of grace, so he gave himself wholly to the priestly work of intercession" (p. 1265).

Another version translates verses 12 and 13: "Epaphras, who is one of your number, a bondslave of Jesus Christ, sends you his greetings, always laboring earnestly for you in his prayers, that you may stand perfect and fully assured in all the will of God. For I bear him witness that he has a deep concern for you and for those who are in Laodicea and Hierapolis" (NASB).

Luke and Demas

In his closing remarks to the Colossians, Paul also referred to Luke: "Luke, the beloved physician" (Col. 4:14). Luke had been a companion of the Apostle Paul on some of his journeys. Luke was also the author of the Gospel of Luke and the Book of the Acts. The relationship between Luke and Paul is seen from Paul's use of the word "beloved." Paul viewed him as more than just a fellow laborer; he was one whom Paul loved.

Along with Luke, Paul mentioned Demas: "Luke, the beloved physician, and Demas, greet you" (v. 14). Here Demas is seen as being with Paul, but later Paul wrote: "Demas hath forsaken me, having loved this present world" (II Tim. 4:10). When Paul wrote to Timothy, he had to say, "Only Luke is with me" (v. 11). But notice his instructions to Timothy: "Take Mark, and bring him with thee: for he is profitable to me for the ministry" (v. 11).

Mark and Demas make an interesting contrast when one studies their lives. On the first missionary journey, Mark had accompanied Paul and Barnabas, but in the midst of the journey, Mark quit and returned home. His full name was John Mark, and Acts 13:13 refers to his leaving Paul and Barnabas to return to Jerusalem. Later, when Paul and Barnabas were about to begin their second missionary journey, Barnabas wanted to take Mark along again, but Paul absolutely refused to do so (see Acts 15:36-41). Second Timothy indicates that Paul later found Mark profitable to him in the ministry (4:11). So Mark first left Paul and later was restored and was profitable to him.

In contrast, Demas was with Paul when Paul communicated the greeting of Demas to the Colossians (Col. 4:14).

However, later when Paul wrote to Timothy, he had to acknowledge that Demas had forsaken him because of his interest in the present world (II Tim. 4:10). How sad to have to say of any believer that he loved the world more than serving Christ and laboring with fellow believers.

Archippus

As Paul concluded his letter to the Colossians, he asked that a special word be passed on to Archippus: "Take heed to the ministry which thou hast received in the Lord, that thou fulfil it" (Col. 4:17). It was uppermost in Paul's mind that he himself might finish the course God had set before him. And since this was his aim, he urged Archippus on to the same goal.

Paul's desire to finish his course is seen from Acts 20:24: "But none of these things move me, neither count I my life dear unto myself, so that I might finish my course with joy, and the ministry, which I have received of the Lord Jesus, to testify the gospel of the grace of God." Paul not only wanted to finish his course, but he wanted to finish it "with joy."

In the last letter we have from Paul's pen, he told Timothy, "I have fought a good fight, I have finished my course, I have kept the faith: henceforth there is laid up for me a crown of righteousness, which the Lord, the righteous judge, shall give me at that day: and not to me only, but unto all them also that love his appearing" (II Tim. 4:7,8).

Paul's word to Archippus in Colossians 4:17 would, of course, apply to all believers. Notice the twofold aspect of Paul's admonition. First, he said, "Take heed to the ministry which thou hast received in the Lord." All of us who know Jesus Christ as Saviour have received a ministry. In a sense, one can say this is part of the salvation package. One not only comes into right relationship with Jesus Christ by faith, but he is also given the responsibility to do something with that message. The Bible says, "And all things are of God, who hath reconciled us to himself by Jesus Christ, and hath given to us the ministry of reconciliation" (II Cor. 5:18). We have already referred to the importance of being faithful in all that God has committed to us (see I Cor. 4:2). Paul also said, "Therefore seeing we have this ministry, as we have received mercy, we faint not" (II Cor. 4:1).

Ephesians 2:8-10 reveals that the outworking of our salvation—good works—is closely tied to salvation itself. Verses 8 and 9 reveal what is involved in salvation: "For by grace are ye saved through faith; and that not of yourselves: it is the gift of God: not of works, lest any man should boast." But notice the expression of that salvation that is to follow: "For we are his workmanship, created in Christ Jesus unto good works, which God hath before ordained that we should walk in them" (v. 10).

The second aspect of Paul's admonition was "take heed to the ministry which thou hast received in the Lord, that thou fulfil it" (Col. 4:17). We are stewards of God because we have been given responsibility concerning the Gospel message. God will someday call for us to give an account of how we have handled our responsibility here on earth: "For we must all appear before the judgment seat of Christ; that every one may receive the things done in his body, according to that he hath done, whether it be good or bad" (II Cor. 5:10). And above all, we will be called into account concerning our faithfulness, as indicated in I Corinthians 4:1,2: "Let a man so account of us, as of the ministers of Christ, and stewards of the mysteries of God. Moreover it is required in stewards, that a man be found faithful."

However, there is great consolation for the work we have to do because when God assigns a task, He also provides all that is necessary to accomplish it. This is seen from Philippians 2. Verse 12 indicates our responsibility: "Work out your own salvation with fear and trembling." But notice that the following verse tells us what God has given us to accomplish this: "For it is God which worketh in you both to will and to do of his good pleasure" (v. 13). In a special sense, ministry is not something we do for God; it is something that God does in and through us. This is apparent from Colossians 1:29: "To this end I labor, struggling with all his energy, which so powerfully works in me" (NIV). Also notice this emphasis from Hebrews 13:21: "Equip you in every good thing to do His will, working in us that which is pleasing in His sight, through Jesus Christ, to whom be the glory forever and ever" (NASB).

Paul's statement referring to the ministry we have received, "that thou fulfil it" (Col. 4:17), shows that God has a definite purpose for every servant. This brings us back to the central theme of the Book of Colossians found in Colossians 2:9,10: "For in him dwelleth all the fulness of the Godhead bodily. And ye are complete in him, which is the head of all principality and power."

The fullness of Jesus Christ is available to every believer. We are complete in Him. He is the all-sufficient Christ!

We have seen from our study of the Book of Colossians that Christ is all that a believer needs—or should ever want—whether for salvation or for the outworking of one's salvation. Beware of any teaching that claims to give us something more than what we already have in Christ. We have a perfect position in Christ because we are complete in Him. And as someone has so well said, "We do not live and grow by addition but by appropriation."

From our study in Colossians, I say to you as Paul said to the Corinthian believers: "God is able to make all grace abound toward you; that ye, always having all sufficiency in all things, may abound to every good work" (II Cor. 9:8). And when you find yourself in spiritual warfare—which is the norm of the Christian life—do not forget the instructions of James 4:7: "Submit yourselves therefore to God. Resist the devil, and he will flee from you."

The Lord Jesus Christ is all we need, for He is the all-sufficient Christ.